PILGRIM FRANCE

Shrines and pilgrim places

by
David Baldwin

To my wife, Ros,
with much love and
huge thanks

All booklets are published thanks to the
generous support of the members of the
Catholic Truth Society

CATHOLIC TRUTH SOCIETY
PUBLISHERS TO THE HOLY SEE

CONTENTS

Destination France 5

Christianity in France..9

Brittany and Normandy 25

    Lisieux 26

    Rouen...34

    Abbey of Mont Saint Michel 40

    St Anne D'Auray 46

    Querrien 49

Centre and Loire Valley 55

    Chartres...56

    Pontmain...66

    Saint-Laurent-Sur-Sèvre 75

    Tours...86

    Solesmes 92

    L'Île Bouchard...95

    Pellevoisin 98

Île de France Paris 101

    Notre Dame...103

    Sacré-Coeur of Montmartre................................111

    Chapel of Our Lady of the Miraculous Medal....118

    Chapel of Saint Vincent de Paul..........................127

La Madeleine 134

St Augustine's Church..139

Burgundy **145**

Nevers...146

Paray-Le-Monial..152

Pontigny..162

Vezelay 164

Cluny 169

Auvergne and Rhône Alps....................................**175**

Ars-Sur-Formans 176

Annecy..181

Chateauneuf-De-Galaure 188

La Salette 195

Laus 199

Lalouvesc..202

Le Puy-En-Velay 205

Pyrenees and Provence **209**

Lourdes 210

Rocamadour..219

Conques 224

La Sainte-Baume 228

Cotignac..234

❧ DESTINATION FRANCE ❧

The convenience, affordability and accessibility of modern travel, combined with proximity just across the Channel, makes France the most popular destination for Britons visiting Europe: some 15 million of us went there in 2007 as visitors or tourists. Apart from the many obvious and wide-ranging sights and attractions, France also offers a wealth of Christian and pilgrim destinations spread right across the country, which reflect her long held Christian tradition – not only as places of awe and beauty in their own right, but also as places of serious and inspirational spirituality. The former may well tempt the casual tourist or visitor, attested by the many millions who visit, for instance, Notre Dame cathedral in Paris, and who quite rightly go for sight, spectacle and a sense of history; the spiritual dimension will tempt the enquiring or the curious, Christian or otherwise, or the seeking pilgrim – as attested by the six million who visit Lourdes annually, to explore or fulfil spiritual needs, felt or unfelt.

But any of these places, for everyone, will give a strong sense of times long past, and the chance to marvel – certainly in a material context – as to the amazing creativity and ingenuity, not to say enormous effort and determination of the people involved in building, re-building and maintaining these beautiful Shrines. On the spiritual side, there permeates a strong feeling of the spirituality and heroism of the people who maintained their faith, sometimes against all odds, which inspires us to immerse ourselves in the atmosphere of prayer of these places, and sense the suffering and joy in which they have been steeped over the centuries.

This book

The purpose of this book is to give a brief highlight of the major (and some lesser) Christian Shrines and Sanctuaries throughout France, with a feel for their history, and where appropriate, something about the people involved. It is aimed at both the casual tourist or visitor to provide some basic information on which to consider a visit, as well as for the spiritual seeker, as an informed 'lead-in' to a more in-depth experience.

It may also be useful for those planning their holiday, for whatever reason they are going, to help finalise or decide a route or destination. As it covers the whole of France, split into geographical areas, it would be a useful companion to your other travel guides, so that as you pass through, or are holidaying in a particular area, it will give you a more specialist flavour of what is there – and at least suggest alternative venues if the weather misbehaves, or as an attractive detour on a long, boring journey: in the words of the Highways Agency's advertisement, 'Don't just drive. Discover!'.

The history and stories of the places and people in this small book are invariably complex and involved. Space precludes no more than a thumbnail – in which I have attempted to distil and highlight the essential and the interesting. My apologies, therefore, in advance, to the more knowledgeable reader, or indeed to the places and people themselves, if they feel I have missed anything of significance. By the same token, I have visited the majority of these destinations, like you – an anonymous visitor and pilgrim – seeking no special treatment or preference. So I have attempted to convey the aura and feel for what I saw and experienced, probably discovering no more than you would on your first visit – leaving just that feeling that it may be worth returning for more!

Practicalities

Rather than clutter the text with internet addresses, which may change anyway, further information on these destinations can be accessed through your favourite search engine. There are also some more-in-depth booklets and Pilgrims' Companions on some of the individual venues in this book that are published by the Catholic Truth Society, and these are listed at the back.

Many of the major Sanctuaries have very reasonable – in price and quality – board and lodging options, and will allow you to stay at the heart of the site, giving an opportunity to mix with local and international travellers and pilgrims, as well as being able to spend quiet times in the grounds or churches when the crowds have gone. Contact details are on their websites, and booking in advance, particularly during busy periods or high season, is recommended.

I have not given too many details of opening times or closed periods, as these too may change or vary with year and season. Suffice it to say most sites are open during 'normal hours' (sometimes beyond), but there are some quirks, like some churches or reception offices being closed over the 'French lunch hour' – it may therefore be worth checking if timing is going to be critical. Travelling by public transport to some locations, particularly the more remote, can pose a bit of a challenge, and may need some research, rather than trying to cuff it!

> *"The real voyage of discovery consists not in seeking new landscapes but in having new eyes."*
>
> Marcel Proust

❧ CHRISTIANITY IN FRANCE ❧

Christianity – and Catholicism – runs long and deep in the history and the psyche of France. In a book of this size and scope it is only possible to give a few impressionist brush strokes of the huge, complex tapestry of Christianity through the centuries: sometimes glorious, sometimes ambivalent, and at other times turbulent and violent.

Because of her very early connections and long involvement with Christianity, France has been described as 'the eldest daughter of the Church', although one modern writer wryly describes her – in the light of her turbulent past, and the perceived secularism of modern Europe – as more 'Prodigal Daughter'; there now may be signs, through the emergence of the many New Movements and signs of renewal, of a Prodigal striving to return to the Father. It is a fascinating, cyclical story of a Church riding the rollercoaster of repression and renewal throughout two millennia – and at one time, during the French Revolution, facing complete annihilation – and yet, always returning in strength, through the dogged faith of her people, encouraged by heroic individuals and Divine events, to renewal and re-growth.

Early centuries

The Christian history of France goes back to the earliest of times, to the very strong tradition that Mary Magdalene, and companions, came to France after the Resurrection, evangelising in the Marseilles area, and ending her days as a hermit in the caves of the Baume Massif in Provence.

Of more historical substance are the accounts of the spread of Christianity westwards and northwards through France – then under Roman rule – during the first three centuries after Our Lord, from such places as Lugdunum, the capital of the Gauls (now Lyons). They tell of Christians being martyred here in 177AD, along with their Bishop Pothinus, indicating an established Christian community, and one holding firm. The early Church Father and apologist St Irenaeus (died c202) and disciple of St Polycarp, succeeded Pothinus as Bishop of Lyons.

The Romans ruled Gaul for nearly 500 years after Christ, and it was from Rome that Christianity continued to spread throughout central and northern Europe. This spread was given huge impetus when the Emperor Constantine declared for religious tolerance throughout the Roman Empire in his Edict of Milan given in 313. One of the indicators of the hold that Christianity had in these early centuries is the 111 or so Gallo-Roman Saints listed before the end of the 5th century – from St Abra of Poitiers, through to St Viventiolus (460–524) one of the Archbishops of Lyons. One of these early Saints of particular note and subsequent influence was the former soldier, St Martin of Tours (316?–397), who instigated a rudimentary parish and pastoral system within his diocese, and was one of the great pioneers of early Western monasticism.

The Roman Empire in Gaul started crumbling in the late third/early fourth centuries through invasion by the so-called barbarians – the Franks, Visigoths and Vandals. The last vestiges fell when the Franks consolidated their hold over Gaul after the Battle of Soissons (486). Again, Christianity benefited from the conversion of a powerful ruler – King Clovis I (466–511), the first King of the Franks, who converted to Catholicism. This act was one of great importance for the Church in western Europe, as Clovis expanded his rule over most of Roman Gaul, giving rise to the Merovingian dynasty, which ruled the Franks for the next two centuries.

Dynastic Eras

The deposition of the last of the Merovingian line, King Childeric III, was instigated by Pope Zachary in 752 in favour of the first monarch of the Carolingian dynasty, Pepin the Short. This gave rise to the beginnings of the Holy Roman Empire – a powerful political coalition of Church and State which sought to rule Europe. Charlemagne (742 – 814), crowned Holy Roman Emperor by Pope Leo III on Christmas Day 800 in the 'old' St Peter's Basilica, was the most prominent of this dynasty, making not only a name for himself as soldier and statesman, but also as a supporter of arts, education and religion, giving rise to a short period of renaissance.

The end of the tenth century saw the disintegration of the Carolingian era and the rise of the Capetian dynasty. Later in this period – the late 11th and mid-12th century – heralded the golden age of monasticism in France, in which St Bernard of Clairvaux (1090 – 1153) was a leading figure. One of the other prominent figures of this era was St Louis – King Louis IX (1214 – 1270) – the only French monarch to be canonised, being considered the ideal Christian ruler, with his piety and kindness to the poor, and his reign of 'just judgement'. He led the unsuccessful Seventh and Eighth Crusades to the Holy Land, spending some years in the Crusader kingdoms.

This turbulent period also saw the continuing and unhealthy entanglement of the Papacy with secular power in Europe, manifested particularly during one stage when the Papacy, under the complete thrall of French monarchs, moved itself from Rome to

Avignon, during the years 1305–1378 (the so called 'Babylonian Captivity'). The lasting effect from this period of partisanship was loss of political power and the spiritual credibility of the Papacy. It also saw the emergence and definition – after the bitter struggles of the Hundred Years War (1337–1453), between the French House of Valois (or Anjou) and the English House of Plantagenet – of France and England as separate nation states.

The spread of Protestantism from the Reformation, sparked by Martin Luther in 1517, came to France in the form of the Huguenots, who through their defamation of Catholicism, were perceived by King Francis I as a threat to the political stability of France. This gave rise to the Wars of Religion (1562–1598), a period of atrocity and violence, culminating in the St Bartholomew's Day massacre in August 1572, when the Catholic party annihilated thousands of Huguenots across France. The Huguenots themselves also wreaked death and destruction in the areas that they occupied. These wars were brought to an end by Henry IV, himself a former Huguenot, through his Edict of Nantes (1598), ensuring tolerance of the Protestant minority, whilst still retaining Catholicism as the official state religion. Ironically, this period also saw the Renaissance, the rebirth of graceful, classical beauty in all its artistic aspects, throughout Europe.

The 17th century saw the apogee of the power of the French monarchy, epitomised by Louis XIV – the Sun King. His, and his extensive court's extravagant and outlandish life at Versailles, and his continual warring, left France in financial and moral peril by the end of his reign, provoking the start of unrest by the bourgeoisie. Ironically, this was also a century of intense spiritual activity, as witnessed by the many notable saints of the time: John Eudes, John Regis, Francis de Sales, Vincent de Paul, Louise de Marillac, Louis de Montfort, Margaret Mary Alacoque and Claude de la Colombière, whose collective legacy still resonates vigorously, throughout France, and the world, today.

Revolution

In the early years of the 18th century the rumblings of discontent amongst the disenfranchised masses grew – fuelled by the writers of the Enlightenment who questioned the class system and the absolutism of the old regime. The climax of this mass disenchantment was the French Revolution, which started in 1789, and of which the epitome was the storming of the Bastille prison – the hated symbol of oppression – on July 14th.

The Revolution, of which a particular episode is described as the 'Reign of Terror', had a profound

The French Revolution.

effect on the Catholic Church, which resonates to this day, as in effect ownership of all Church property, including churches, was taken by the State, and all priests and religious willing to serve the new regime were paid and appointed as state employees; religious orders were dissolved and dispersed. All priests and religious were required to swear loyalty to the Civil Constitution of the Clergy – there was widespread refusal to do this, which led to exile, deportations and executions. Pope Pius VI did not accept the Constitution, further isolating those that supported it.

One episode of particular note, was the War in the Vendée (1793–96), the coastal region south of the Loire in western France. The people of this area – where there was little resentment against what was an impoverished local nobility – all doggedly clung to their Catholic faith, being led from the front with 153 bishops out of 160, and about half their parish priests, refusing to swear to the Civil Constitution. Retribution was severe: under the banner of 'pacification', the Republican forces defeated the Vendéan – mainly peasant – army in a series of battles, and effected a scorched earth policy, during which tens of thousands of Vendéans were put to the sword. For nearly two hundred years until modern times, this uprising was taught in French history as one against taxes and conscription, with no reference to its religious origins.

Apart from the violent effect that the Revolution had on the people of the Church, the pilgrim places described in this book, along with all other churches and religious buildings, were 'de-Christianised'. Much religious imagery was destroyed, and the buildings were handed over to secular purposes for use as warehouses, stabling, accommodation or factories, or demolished and used as building material. With this physical destruction and wilful desecration, efforts were also made to eradicate the influence of the Church and its practices altogether, with civic festivals replacing religious ones, and the establishment of the so-called Cult of Reason. The subsequent restoration of these buildings to their former glory, from humblest church to majestic cathedral, speaks much of the resilience of the Church and the faith and determination of its people to continue giving glory to God in public places of worship.

Church reinstated

The Revolution ended in 1799 with Napoleon Bonaparte declaring himself Emperor – inaugurating the Napoleonic era. Napoleon, realising that de-Christianisation had caused chaos, confusion and deep division, reversed the process with his Concordat of 1801. This reinstated Catholicism, recognising it as the religion (but not the 'official religion') of the great majority of France, and at the same time restoring a closer relationship with the Papacy, but overall control of Church affairs was still tied very closely to the state.

If the 17th century could be described as the era of great French saints inspiring renewal from within, then the post-Revolution 19th century can be summed up as the era of divine intervention, with the Marian apparitions inspiring renewal from outwith: Rue de Bac, La Salette, Lourdes, Pontmain and Pellevoisin.

As the Napoleonic Era drew to a close, France stood on the threshold of the 20th century as a Republic, and again, the question of the Church's standing within the State came to the fore. The 1880s saw the expulsion of thousands of priests from the schools in which they were teaching, and the closing down, expulsion and exile of religious orders, many of whom came and established their houses in the British Isles. 1902–1905 saw a Radical Socialist government with a particularly virulent anti-clerical policy, with further closures of Catholic schools and foundations and further expulsion of religious orders.

This period culminated in the declaration of the Law on the Separation of the Churches and the State, in 1905. This established the public principle of *laïcité*, the neutrality of the state with respect to religious doctrines, and the separation of religious and public affairs. Bizarrely, though, all church buildings in existence up until 1905 remain to this day under state ownership, and are maintained by the public purse – national or local, depending on the status and location of the church.

But of course, eclipsing all this was the cataclysm of two World Wars, which was to further test the Church in France.

People and Places

Woven into this vast historic tapestry are the heroic people of the Church in France – those known and unknown – who either prospered or suffered, depending on their and the Church's circumstances at their time. Many are covered in this book – such as those saints who lived and died in anonymity and obscurity, but whose legacy subsequently emerged to give glory to God on a global scale. People like the enclosed nun, St Margaret Mary Alacoque, who through her visions of the Sacred Heart of Jesus, brought to the world a wide exposure to this devotion; and St Thérèse of Lisieux, the Little Flower of Jesus, who brought to us, through her profound writings, a whole new way of life; St Catherine Labouré, from her Parisian convent, revealed Our Lady's desire to propagate the devotion of the Miraculous Medal. Also amongst the obscure is a woman of our own time, the

Servant of God Marthe Robin, mystic and stygmatic, who spent her long life crippled and bedridden, never moving from her home in the rural depths of the Rhone-Alps, but through her humble but powerful ministry, had an enormous and lasting influence on the renewal of the Church in France in the late 20th century, and on into the present.

Then from the obscure, to those towering public figures, who proclaimed their mission tirelessly and fearlessly: St Jean Vianney, the Curé of Ars, devoted and selfless parish priest; the 'vagabond priest', intellectual and mendicant, St Louis de Montfort, champion of Our Lady, leaving behind him a solid, worldwide legacy; the intellectual and fearless preacher and Doctor of the Church, St Francis de Sales; the impish looking but unstinting servant of the poor and the sick, St Vincent de Paul, again leaving a worldwide legacy of ministering, in his name to the poor and the vulnerable.

Then there are the children – the visionaries – unworldly, poor, uneducated, obscure, and on the face of it, less than credible, but nonetheless, chosen by God as His messengers through the Apparitions of Our Lady, such as St Bernadette of Lourdes; the shepherd children of La Salette, Laus and Querrien; the schoolchildren of Pontmain.

In a league of her own was St Joan of Arc: illiterate, peasant child and a teenager when she was martyred; mystic and visionary, towering and inspiring public figure and fearless warrior, who led France's army to victories, under God's direction.

Another group of people of more modern times worth highlighting are the French Catholic intellectuals of the late 19th and early 20th centuries. They instigated an upsurge of intellectual debate, fuelled by what Dr James Hitchcock (Professor of History at St Louis University) proposes the "necessary confrontation with a hostile culture which was a permanent feature of Catholic life (in France)", and their purpose was "appropriation of mediaeval thought for modern use". For instance, Jacques Maritain was notable in his revival of the works of Thomas Aquinas, and was a prominent drafter of the Universal Declaration of Human Rights. Ironically many of these were converts to Catholicism – Jacques and Raissa Maritain, Léon Bloy, and Charles Péguy; also prominent amongst them were Henri Bergson and the composer Oliver Messiaen.

"We do not need a truth to serve us, we need a truth that we can serve."

Jacques Maritain

Outlasting the people of those times however, are the glorious church buildings that abound over France. Between 1170 and 1270 eighty cathedrals and nearly 500 major churches were constructed. They were built in times of low technology, leaving one wondering how they were ever designed, let alone constructed – from the minute, intricate detail, to the immense, gracious grandeur. The iconic Notre Dame, the spiritually charged and beautiful Sacre-Coeur in Montmartre, Chartres cathedral, the absolute epitome of what French Academician Georges Dubuy meant in describing beautiful churches as 'a place where God and man could meet… a sort of anteroom to Paradise…'. The Basilica at Pontmain must also rate well in this category, with its stunning acres of modern, luminous, stained-glass windows; and, in complete contrast, the simple church in a cliff-side cave at La Sainte-Baume.

A Marian Nation

But above all, France is a Marian nation, being the recipient of many apparitions of Our Lady – from the oldest at Cotignac, Provence in 1519 (Our Lady of Graces), to the latest at L'Île Bouchard, Centre, in 1947 (Our Lady of Prayer). The best known throughout the Christian world is, of course, Lourdes (1858), where Our Lady appeared to the young peasant girl Bernadette, and is now a major sanctuary, being visited by some six million people every year, seeking healing and hope. With all these appearances, here is Our Lady – Mother of the Universal Church – showing special concern to France, her eldest daughter.

Cardinal François Richard, Archbishop of Paris, summed up all the foregoing beautifully and succinctly as he prayed in Notre Dame Cathedral, Paris, in 1893:

This church has been associated with all the joys and sorrows of our nation: here, we have celebrated our most glorious triumphs, we have mourned our greatest disasters. During the time of our most reprehensible straying, we replaced the cult of sacrilege with the adoration of your Son Jesus; and, when you granted us mercy, your people came back to your feet to recognise you as its Mother and its Queen.

O, Our Lady of Paris, in the name of all these memories, in the name of the maternal love you have always had for Paris and for France, we pray that you will keep in our souls the love of Jesus Christ and His Church! Defend us from the spread of impiety and vice; allow us to remain your children who love you! Give us Saints who will return to us the faith and virtue of days gone by.

O Queen, O Mother, kneeling before your image, at the very spot where the Saints, our fathers, and the protectors of our France, so often invoked your name, we hope to pray as they did, and to live and to die as they did. Answer our prayers! Amen.

BRITTANY
～ AND NORMANDY ～

LISIEUX

*"Love proves itself by deeds, so how am I to show
my love? Great deeds are forbidden me. The only
way I can prove my love is by scattering flowers,
and these flowers are every little sacrifice, every
glance and word, and the doing of the least
actions for love." St Thérèse of Lisieux*

The Town of Lisieux

Lisieux is a small, charming rural town in Normandy,
close to the coastal holiday resorts of Côte Fleurie,
and about an hour's drive from the Channel ferry
ports of Le Havre and Caen. The gentle, rolling
countryside is very reminiscent of rural, farming
England, and the area is well known for its smooth
Calvados, handsome chateaux and tasty cheeses! It is
a major pilgrim destination, as pilgrims from all over
the world come here to venerate and seek the
intercession of its exalted daughter, Thérèse Martin,
the canonised Carmelite nun, St Thérèse of the Child
Jesus and the Holy Face – also affectionately known
as the Little Flower of Jesus.

In times past, Thomas Becket, Henry II's
Archbishop of Canterbury, took refuge here for a
period during his seven years exile. It was an area of
continuing dispute in the tangled conflicts of the

English and French monarchies during the Hundred Years War. But it saw its biggest upheaval immediately after the D-Day landings, as a significant part of the town was destroyed during the Allied advance. However, despite the bombardments and fierce fighting, all those places associated with Thérèse – the nearly completed Basilica, the Cathedral, the Carmel and her family home – were left largely unscathed. There are also a few remaining half-timbered medieval buildings still standing, giving a hint of the old town.

St Thérèse

Thérèse was born in 1873 in the French town of Alençon, the youngest child of a family of nine. It was a pious (in the best sense!) and devoted family – all the five surviving sisters entered convents – and just recently, in October 2008, Thérèse's parents, Louis and Zélie Martin, were beatified by Pope Benedict XVI – the only married couple, to my knowledge, earning this unique recognition within the context of marriage and family life.

The death of Thérèse's mother from breast cancer when Thérèse was four, provoked a family move to the nearby town of Lisieux. This death of a parent had a profound effect on Thérèse's early childhood, and she gradually withdrew and sickened to the point that family and friends feared for her life: it was only through the powerful and telling intercession of Our Lady that she was healed.

Thérèse's calling to the religious life was something she felt very strongly, very early on. Against great opposition from senior clergy, but with strong support from her father, she was accepted into the Carmelite convent at Lisieux at the tender age of fifteen. After she had settled to convent life and made her Final Profession it was obvious to the other Sisters that here was a person young in years, but profound in her spirituality. Under obedience to her Prioress, she was required to write about her early life and her spiritual thoughts.

After only nine years in Carmel, aged twenty four, Thérèse died of an agonising form of tuberculosis. It was only when her profound spiritual writings – *Histoire d'une Âme* (The Story of a Soul) – gradually emerged to the world, and with them the manifestation of the many miracles and conversions associated with her intercession, that the significance of her ministry was realised.

She was canonised in May 1925 by Pope Pius XI; in December 1927 she was proclaimed by Pius as Patroness of Missions. In October 1997 she was declared a Doctor of the Church by Pope John Paul II – the youngest, and only the third woman. Her feast day throughout the Universal Church is 1st October. Having lived and died in complete obscurity, Thérèse's wish of being a missionary, was, by the grace of God, fulfilled. Her writings have spread worldwide, and her relics have visited over forty nine countries, including England and Wales, bringing great graces and favours to all those places.

"I want to spend my heaven doing good upon earth... I shall let fall a shower of roses".

Pilgrim Places in Lisieux

Basilica of St Thérèse: This massive church, built in neo-Byzantine style, with its dome, turrets, slender windows and gracious arches, was paid for entirely from public subscription, being started in 1929 and consecrated in 1954. Its sturdy construction survived the D-Day Allied bombings, and the intervention of a British major in the advancing forces averted serious damage, when he advised that it was not being defended by the Germans. In all, it is an impressive tribute to this young nun, but it is the inside, with its staggering 8,000 square metres of mosaics, in a bold, contemporary style – a lot of which depicts aspects of Thérèse's life – that will hold your attention. In complete contrast to the bright mosaics of the main church are the subtle, muted and exquisite mosaics in the large, arched Crypt. Here also lie the remains of Thérèse's parents, Louis and Zélie, and off the Crypt, a quiet, understated and tranquil Blessed Sacrament Chapel. There is a sweet waxwork diorama portraying Thérèse's life, under the left hand church cloister. Under the right hand cloister is a cinema, which shows a film on Thérèse's life. Opposite the church, across the parvis, is a large modern Pastoral Reception Centre, with bookshop and facilities. The unusual obelisk standing well clear of the church is the campanile or bell tower, housing the 51 bells – it is a treat if you get to hear them playing their intricate, delicate and sonorous tunes.

Cathedral of St Peter: The dignified, graceful, but rather careworn cathedral, distinct with its two mismatched towers, which has probably not changed much since Thérèse's day, is where the Martin family regularly worshipped, and is set near the centre of the town. It is built in the Gothic style, being started in the 12th century, and completed in the 13th and 16th centuries. Inside it is plain, with no profusion of statuary or carving, or stunning stained glass windows – but this gives it a chance to exhibit its exquisite architecture, with its three pillared and arched naves and numerous side chapels. In it there is visible evidence of Thérèse's and the Martin family's involvement: the confessional where Thérèse made her first confession, the intricately carved, white marble high altar given by Thérèse's father as a votive offering in 1888, and the side chapel in the right hand ambulatory, which was rented by the Martin family for Sunday Mass, and in which there is a modern statue of the young Thérèse praying.

Les Buissonnets: Les Buissonnets (The Thicket, or Bushes) is the Martin family house, of which Thérèse described it as 'this beautiful cradle of my childhood'. It is a few minutes walk from the cathedral. It is a charming, warm red-brick, late 18th century house, with attractive pale stone mullions framing the numerous windows, surrounded by small, neat gardens. One enters directly into the large, homely, family kitchen. Next door is the family dining room, furnished as it was, including the clock above the fireplace made by Thérèse's father, Louis, a clock maker by profession. Upstairs you can view the family bedrooms, in which one is a copy of the statue of Our Lady 'of the smile', through which Thérèse's healing came; and in another, a display of Thérèse's childhood toys, dolls, clothes and knick-knacks – a fascinating snapshot of a middle class childhood from a God-fearing family of that era. Taking pride of place is Thérèse's First Holy Communion dress with adornments and rosary. Outside is a small, cosy garden, in which is a statue of Thérèse kneeling before her father, pleading her case to enter the Carmelite convent.

Carmel: Carmel, where Thérèse spent the rest of her short life, is again close to the town centre, quietly set back from the rue de Carmel. The chapel is a small, unadorned, simple church, with only the statues of St John of the Cross and St Teresa of Avila on display. Here, you can join with the Sisters as they take their place in the choir for Mass or Daily Office – a beautiful and serene experience listening to their prayer and singing, accompanied by one of the Sisters playing a zither. Just off to the right of the chapel is the semi-circular, domed side chapel containing St Thérèse's relics. In a large, ornate, glass fronted reliquary (*chasse*) is the recumbent, peaceful figure, fashioned in marble and precious wood, of Thérèse on her death bed. Above the reliquary is the original statue of the Virgin 'of the smile': a peaceful scene, which radiates beauty and serenity. On the other side of the chapel is the *parcours Thérèsien:* a modern and appealing display area, showing aspects, and artifacts, of Thérèse's life, and that of a Carmelite nun.

The Carmel - Reliquary, and above, the statue of the 'Virgin of the smile'.

"My life is but an instant, a passing hour,
My life is but a day that escapes and flies away.
Oh my God! You know that to love you on earth
I only have today!"

From St Thérèse's 'My Song for Today'

ROUEN

"One life is all we have, and we live it as we
believe in living it. But to sacrifice what you are
and to live without belief, that is a fate more
terrible than dying." Joan of Arc

Rouen, some 90 kms directly east of the cross-Channel ferry port of Le Havre, is the capital of Upper Normandy, and the fourth largest port in France, straddling the River Seine. It was described by Victor Hugo as the city of a hundred spires, which sadly may not be the case today, as it was extensively damaged during World War II. Restoration since then has been painstaking, particularly in the centre, much of which has been reconstructed in the mediaeval style. In the context of this book, though, it is about St Joan of Arc – the intriguing, enigmatic and heroic martyr – burned at the stake for heresy, here in Rouen in 1431, aged just nineteen.

Saint Joan of Arc

Joan of Arc was born circa 1412 in the village of Domrémy, eastern France, of a peasant family – d'Arc being her father's family name. From aged about twelve she claimed that she had visions and heard voices, which included instructions from God to lead the armies in driving the English out of France, and to take the Dauphin, the future Charles VII, to English-occupied Reims, and have him crowned King. As an unknown, uneducated, teenage peasant girl, being taken seriously was very difficult, but her persistence won through, particularly when her specific prediction of a military victory came about.

With her credibility (and spirituality) thus established, she was permitted to attend war planning councils. And then, at the head of the French army, with her utter faith in God and employing daring tactics – wearing her armour and carrying her banner aloft – she was instrumental in lifting the long-standing siege of Orléans, and was soon dubbed 'the Maid of Orléans'. In leading a series of campaigns up the Loire to Reims, she fulfilled the goal of taking the city from the English and was present at the coronation of Charles VII in Reims cathedral in July 1429.

Her continuing military forays, particularly the attack on Paris, however, started to founder, mainly through apathy and lack of support from the King and his advisers. In May 1430 she was eventually captured in fighting at Compiègne. She was abandoned by the French to her fate. The English were delighted at having taken such a prestigious captive, and after two trials before ecclesiastical courts, she was found guilty of being a 'relapsed heretic', for which the sentence was being burned to death at the stake.

Her demeanour at her execution, held in May 1431 in the Old Market Place in Rouen, was reported to have moved the strongest to tears; she called for a crucifix and after embracing it, kept her eyes fixed on it, continuously calling the name of Jesus. Her ashes were thrown into the Seine to prevent any veneration of a martyr's relics.

Twenty four years later a trial of nullification was held in Paris with the consent of the Holy See, principally on the grounds of the doubtful legality in canon law of the original trials. The findings against her were reversed. The cause for her beatification was taken up in 1869 by the Bishop of Orléans; she was canonised in 1920 by Pope Benedict XV. She is one of the five patron saints of France, the patron of soldiers, and her feast day is celebrated on the 30th May.

Pilgrim places in Rouen

Joan's Rouen is quite walkable, and a brochure 'In the Footsteps of Joan of Arc' is available from the Tourist Information Office opposite Rouen cathedral.

Church of St Joan of Arc: The place most associated with St Joan in Rouen is the Old Market Square (*place du Vieux Marché*) where she was martyred, and in which this striking, modern church was built in 1979. Its unusual architecture harmonises with the small indoor market, built next door at the same time: the saw-tooth roofs of the market place conjuring up images of waves (or, to me, sails), and the twisting, rearing, trapezoidal, slate covered roof of the church – variously an upturned boat or keel, or, when viewed in the round with the stained glass windows below, flames – presents a dramatic picture. The interior is just as striking – the congregation is placed in semi-circle facing the main altar, against whose dramatic backdrop is a vibrant wall of 16th century stained glass windows, rescued from the nearby church of St Vincent before it was destroyed during World War II. Looking up at the nave roof, the nautical theme is again emphasized with its resemblance to an upturned hull. The Blessed Sacrament side chapel has the original panelling from St Vincent's church, and is a

Church of St Joan of Arc.

quiet, reflective place to pray. There is a bookshop inside the church. Close by the church is the Joan of Arc museum, and also shown is the area where Joan was put to death, indicated by the signs *'Le Bucher'* and *'Pilori'*.

Cathedral of Notre Dame: The present Gothic cathedral was started in the 12th century and largely completed in the 13th century, being the third church on this site – the first dating from the 4th century. It had the very secular distinction of being the tallest building in the world between 1876 and 1880, with the spikey, tapering, needle-spire of the central Lantern Tower reaching skywards to 151m above the ground. One of the two mismatching front façade towers was built from donations by wealthy citizens in return for being allowed to eat butter during Lent – fittingly it is called the Butter Tower! Claude Monet painted many pictures of the exterior of the cathedral, showing delicate displays of light in differing conditions, playing over the complex architecture. Inside, the central nave has a lofty four storey elevation, flanked by the serried ranks of pillars and arches, giving into the side naves. The stained glass windows represents art periods ranging from the Middle Ages to early Renaissance. Off the right hand nave is a side chapel dedicated to St Joan, with a statue of her at the stake, and modern stained glass windows depicting her life. A sword, on the altar front, bisects the names 'JESVS' and 'MARIA'.

ABBEY OF MONT SAINT MICHEL

"....my eyes fastened on this gigantic jewel, as big as a mountain, cut like a cameo, and as dainty as lace..."

Guy de Maupassant

Probably one of the most evocative, most romantic and most visited pilgrim sites outside Paris and excluding Lourdes, is the Abbey of Mont Saint Michel – sitting just off the coast, in the estuary between Brittany and Normandy. It seems to rise mysteriously out of the sea – a small pyramidal island acutely accented by the tall, tapering spire of the abbey church, forming the delicate apex. It is intriguing that but a short distance across the sea to the Cornish coast, sits the mirror image of its namesake – St Michael's Mount.

History

This small, granite island, surrounded as it was by treacherous tides and currents, was a natural stronghold position. In the 6th and 7th centuries it was

The Abbey of Mont Saint Michel.

an American fortification of Romano-Breton culture and power, engaging in cross-channel dealings after the Roman departure in the 5th century; this role was terminated by the subsequent Frankish invasion and occupation.

The first religious building on this site was a monastery built – according to legend in response to the promptings of St Michael the Archangel – by St Aubert, Bishop of Avranches, commencing in about 708. In 1017 Abbot Hildebert II began a colossal and ambitious building scheme to build up a platform level with the summit on which a new abbey would stand. The link with St Michael's Mount in Cornwall came about in 1067, when the abbey was granted properties and land, which included the island off the Cornish coast, by William of Normandy for the support they gave to his claim to the English throne.

The great building scheme initiated by Hildebert persevered for many centuries and against many problems – constructional and political – until final completion of the major works of the dramatic abbey choir in 1520. Part of this ongoing construction was the addition of the Marvel (*le Merveille*) on the north side of the abbey in the 13th century, consisting principally of the refectory, the knights' hall and the supporting undercroft.

As a result of the decline of monastic life in the late 16th century the fortunes of the monastery diminished. During the French Revolution the abbey was used as a prison, the whole being returned to the French Government in 1874 for restoration by the Centre of Historic Monuments. It is a UNESCO World Heritage Site. The Monastic Fraternities of Jerusalem are resident in the abbey, ensuring a continuing religious community and spiritual presence.

Visiting

The island is connected by a causeway; parking is available adjacent to the causeway – dictated by the state of the tides, of which clear direction and indication is given! You cannot help but wonder at the amazing sight of this beautiful complex looming above you as you approach, with its unique combination of delicacy and strength, in this improbable location. It is a compact, steep site, so, in busy times be prepared for throngs, as well as for a steep climb up many steps.

As you enter through the Burgher's Guardroom and go through the King's Gate, where the portcullis is, you will see why this island was so impregnable to attack, with its massive fortifications, and above, the commanding ramparts – defying the best efforts of the English attackers in the Hundred Years War. A steady walk up the Grande Rue will start orientating you to the Mount, with its narrow confines and multitude of shops and food outlets, clustered at the foot of the abbey buildings, and leading on up to the abbey. About halfway up on the left is the charming mediaeval **parish church of St Pierre**, with a side chapel housing a powerful statue of St Michael. Close to this church is the **Maison du Pelerin**, the pilgrim office (and shop).

Abbey

Once in the abbey confines, a simple guide brochure, or the audio guide, will conduct you round this gloriously confusing and varied conglomeration of buildings and spaces. The abbey church is quite austere, but with its soaring Gothic arches, and light pouring in from the high clerestory windows round the sanctuary, emanates grace and beauty. There is a Blessed Sacrament chapel reserved for quiet prayer. Mass is celebrated daily. One of the rewards of your climb will be the wide, glorious views of the coastline and countryside from the abbey's terrace, and a chance to marvel at the layers of buildings clinging to the island, and to gaze up to the slender steeple, atop which sits the gilded statue of St Michael.

In your wanderings you will come across the classic four-sided abbey cloister, with its wide, covered walkway and surround of delicate twin pillars and exquisitely sculpted arches, all enclosing a lawned and hedged garden; the magnificent Gothic interior of the Knights' Hall; the simplicity of the large, barrel-ceilinged refectory, with its 'hidden' windows (presumably obscuring the views so as to not distract the monks from listening to the readings at their silent mealtimes!); the ingenious and huge human treadmill winch for lifting heavy loads; the mighty pillars supporting the abbey sanctuary from below – and of course the ubiquitous presence of St Michael the Archangel. You will always be conscious of the surrounding sea and vista, visible through the many apertures and windows as you go round.

There is a good day's worth of gentle 'pilgrimaging' here, if you want to take in the detail and the grandeur, not only of the abbey confines, but also the wider opportunities of exploring the ramparts and the town below, without feeling too pressurised, as well as to immerse yourself in the history and spirituality, so that in every way you may appreciate this extraordinary place.

ST ANNE D'AURAY

"I am Anne, the mother of Mary. There was a chapel here before that was dedicated to me. I ask you to build it again, and to take care of it, because God wants me to be honoured here."

In south Brittany, some 50 kms east of Lorient, off the N165/E60 and just north of the town of Auray, is the village of St Anne d'Auray. Here, between 1623 and 1625, Our Lady's mother, Anne, appeared to Yves Nicolazic, a farm labourer. It is a popular place of pilgrimage, and like many of these small French pilgrimage villages, is dominated by a magnificent Basilica – this one being dedicated to St Anne.

Apparitions

St Anne was first venerated here from the 6th century, a small chapel being built and dedicated to her by early Christians. Although this chapel was subsequently destroyed by fire, the village name 'Keranna' – 'village of Anne' in Breton – lived on.

In August 1623, as they were taking their oxen to water, Yves Nicolazic and his brother-in-law saw a majestic lady, filled with radiant light – but who did not speak. Although the men were amazed by this appearance they were reluctant to act upon it. Nearly a year later in July 1624 the lady appeared again to Yves, asking him to build a chapel in her honour. Again Yves chose to try and ignore this appearance. One evening in March 1625, the apparition came to Yves in the form of a single burning candle, also witnessed by his neighbours. The candle led them to the site of the former chapel, where buried in the ground they discovered an ancient statue of St Anne.

After a thorough episcopal investigation of these claims, the Bishop of Vannes recognised their validity and authorised the chapel to be built in 1625. As again, with many of these apparition sites, that chapel soon became too small to cope with pilgrim numbers.

Basilica of St Anne

The current basilica was built of granite between 1865 and 1872, being described as a mix of Gothic boldness and Renaissance elegance. It has an extensive frontage and parvis, with well kept gardens and grounds. The basilica is dominated at the lower level by the large rose window on the entrance façade, and then your eye is taken upwards, to the tall, elegant and intricate tower and steeple, topped by a bronze statue of St Anne, holding a flaming torch aloft. On the basilica approach is the fountain, capped by the statue of St Anne and Our Lady, where Yves had his first apparition. Adjacent to the fountain is the World War I war memorial to the

Basilica of St Anne D'Auray.

Bretons who gave their lives, and across the lawn from the front of the Basilica is the Santa Scala – the Holy Stairs – that formed part of the previous chapel.

Inside, the long graceful, arched naves, with, just to the left as you enter, the remains of Yves Nicolazic, beneath the St Yves' altar. The south (right) arm of the transept houses the altar of St Anne. The original statue found by Yves was destroyed during the French Revolution; a fragment of it is embedded in the altar plinth. A replacement statue, carved in 1825, sits in the altar niche. A statue of Yves also stands at this altar. A fragment of St Anne's arm, brought back from Constantinople from the Crusades and presented by Louis XIII, is in the reliquary in the left hand transept.

The reconstructed house of Yves Nicolazic is close to the Information Office, and gives a good feel for life in a Keranna cottage of the 17th century.

QUERRIEN

"We come to you today at Querrien. We come from all the villages in our land of Brittany and the most distant countries. We'll meet in these places where St. Gall announced the Good News of Jesus Christ… We come as pilgrims, O Mary, show us the path that leads to Jesus."

From the prayer to our Lady of All Help

The small village of Querrien, buried in the heart of rural southern Brittany – in the department of Finisterre, 13 kms directly north of Quimperle – must be one of the best kept secrets amongst approved apparitions of Our Lady. It does not appear on any of the apparition lists of my researches, and it was only through casual conversation with a priest friend, that this little gem emerged!

The parish of Querrien is intriguingly named after St Kerien, reportedly a Welshman, born in the first half of the 5th century. Having helped found a monastery in Cleder, North Brittany, he sought solitude in a hermitage at Querrien, soon building up a community that dwelt there. Later, leaving his community, he returned to Cleder, where he died in 490. The Irishman, St Gall, who accompanied St Columbanus to Gaul, is also reported to have founded a chapel and an oratory here in 610, leaving in it a carved statue – all of which were destroyed or lost in the mists of history.

Jeanne Courtel

Over a thousand years later, in August 1652, Jeanne Courtel, an eleven year old deaf and dumb shepherdess, was tending her sheep. Our Lady appeared to her asking for one of her lambs. Her natural reply was this was not for her to give, as they belonged to her father. On being reassured by Our

Lady that she would tend her sheep, Jeanne rushed home to tell her father of the encounter. Her parents were astonished, as she could now hear and speak. On being asked what else Our Lady had told her, she replied that her wish was to have a chapel built in the village to bring in many pilgrims to honour her, and that a long lost and forgotten statue carved by St Gall should be recovered from a nearby pond – where it had been lying for over a thousand years.

In September of 1652 the Bishop of Saint-Brieuc, having investigated the apparition, declared it to be worthy of belief and authenticated it. The chapel was built between 1652 and 1656, in which lies the tomb of Jeanne, who died in 1703. The chapel was enlarged in 1779. In 1950 more than 20,000 pilgrims gathered with the bishops of Brittany to crown the statue of Our Lady of All Help. Various associated works have been ongoing to accommodate the ever-increasing numbers of pilgrims, with the Cardinal Archbishop of Paris blessing the new buildings in 2000. Major reconciliation ceremonies and processions ('hours-of-pardons') are held here in August, September and October.

Shrine of Our Lady of All Help

The small chapel and Shrine to Our Lady of All Help has a charm and simplicity that exudes its 17th

The Shrine of Our Lady of All Help.

century heritage, and has probably not changed much since it was first built. It is a humble, bluff building with an exterior of rough, undressed stonework, fronted by its square, blunt tower, topped by a small conical steeple. Its few windows give little away as to what lies inside. Inside, the apse is centred on the crowned statue of Our Lady, in a bright poly-chromed, be-statued setting, above the tabernacle and high altar. The two side altars in the transept continue this vibrant theme. One of the stained glass windows depicts the apparition scene. This unassuming little church sums up the simplicity – but also the majesty and dignity – of Our Lady's appearance here, which now lives on, through this Shrine, through the centuries.

Just outside the church is the **fountain of St Gall**, and a bit further away the **field of apparition** and the **miraculous fountain**. **Espace John Paul II** houses the modern pilgrim centre, and there is a small pilgrim hostel nearby.

CENTRE AND
❧ LOIRE VALLEY ❧

CHARTRES

"This has been standing here for centuries – the premier work of man perhaps in the whole western world. And it's without a signature! Chartres! A celebration to God's glory and the dignity of man... Ours, the scientists keep telling us, is a universe which is disposable. You know it might be just this one anonymous glory, of all things, this rich stone forest, this epic chant, this gaiety, this grand choiring shout of affirmation, which we choose when all our cities are dust; to stand intact, to mark where we have been, to testify to what we had it in us to accomplish".

Orson Welles

Chartres

The small city of Chartres, located on the Plain of Beauce, 'the granary of France', is some 90 kms south west from the centre of Paris, enabling a convenient day visit, particularly by train, just an hour away. Tens of thousands of pilgrims and visitors come here every year to marvel at the wonders of what must be one of the most beautiful and elegant churches in the world – the Gothic cathedral dedicated to Our Lady. Because of the flat plain, early evidence of this beauty

can be seen on some of the approaches to the town –
the graceful spires and bulk of the cathedral
seemingly floating above the surrounding
countryside. The cathedral is designated a UNESCO
World Heritage site.

Chartres is also a charming place. It is located on
the three-way split of the River Eure, crossed by
several bridges, some ancient. The old town of half-
timbered houses, water mills and wash houses
provides a glimpse into a world past. For stained glass
enthusiasts there are two other churches of interest: **St
Aignan's** and **St Pierre's Abbey** church, as well as
the **International Stained Glass Centre**. Close to the
cathedral are a park and a fine-arts museum housed in
the splendour of a former episcopal palace.

Chartres Cathedral

The present magnificent edifice is not only testament
to the pioneering architects, skilled artisans and
builders of the day, but also to the tenacity and
determination of the local bishops and people, as the
three previous churches between the 4th and 11th
centuries on the site had been destroyed by fire. The
present cathedral took nearly two centuries to emerge
in its final form, construction having been started by
St Fulbert, the then Bishop of Chartres, in the early
11th century.

Sadly, Fulbert's completed efforts were almost obliterated by fire in 1194, in which and more devastatingly was the apparent loss of the *Sancta Camisia*, the Holy Veil of Our Lady, reputed to be the garment worn when Mary gave birth to Our Lord, and presented to Chartres by the Holy Roman Emperor in 876. Miraculously the Veil emerged unscathed from the devastation of the fire. This spurred a concerted and determined donatory and building effort from the King downwards to provide an even more splendid offering to the glory of God.

The bulk of the current building, incorporating what remained of Fulbert's church, swiftly took shape between 1194 and 1220, finally being re-consecrated in 1260. This relatively short, major construction period accounts for the cathedral's consistent and uniform Gothic style, setting high standards for those seeking to emulate it – such as Reims and Amiens. The design also pioneered the flying buttress – that highly practical and visually attractive architectural device – not only enabling taller structures, but also allowing more space for larger window apertures, of which Notre Dame in Paris is now the iconic embodiment.

Minor works took place thereafter, the most obvious and notable was the addition of the intricate and delicate Gothic spire (North or left hand) at the beginning of the 16th century. It was one of the few churches that was spared any major destruction or looting during the French Revolution – the townsfolk prevented any such moves, including defying instructions to destroy the whole building by explosive demolition.

Exterior

Before entering any of these places it maybe worth taking a slow walk round the outside, mainly to start getting an overall impression and feel, but also to savour the anticipation of what awaits within. You will more than likely approach the cathedral across the parvis, to the west front – in effect the main entrance. Despite its overall symmetry, what may strike you is the two mismatched spires of the west front, adding a quirky charm to this stately building. The north tower is usually available to ascend, affording wide views of the surrounding country, as well as hitherto unseen details of the town and cathedral.

One of the notable exterior features of the cathedral is its major entrance portals on three sides. Adorning them is an immense profusion of statues of all sizes – ranked in lines, singly, or processing round curved archways, embellished with intricate and detailed surrounds.

As you get closer to the west front, the detail of the enormous, be-statued entrance doors on the Royal or West portal will start to emerge. This concentrates on depicting the Nativity, the Ascension, and in the centre, Christ in His Majesty of the Second Coming. The statues here are more worn by time and weather – not surprising – they have been here since the middle of the 12th century!

On continuing round the outside clockwise you will start to notice the chunky, stepped, nave buttresses at the lower level – and then, on looking upwards, you will see them as they 'fly'. I also rather liked the lovely little finishing touch of the standing statues atop each of the solid abutments – peeping out from their niches.

You will then come across the North Portal (early 13th century), the one that took my fascination the most. I was particularly struck by the clarity and explicitness – not only with the carving, but also the depiction and symbolism of the Old Testament prophets: Melchizedek, Abraham, Moses, Samuel, David, Isaiah, Jeremiah; and, linking to the New Testament, Simeon, the emaciated figure of John the Baptist, and Peter, opposite Melchizedek, his chalice broken – the link between Old and New.

Going on round you will now see the far more explicit and delicate flying buttresses that support the choir (sanctuary) area. Also at this top end of the church there is a sizeable and pleasant gravel and tree-lined terrace overlooking the old town – ideal for a relax and a picnic. Lastly, going on round, is the South Portal, with its many exquisitely carved statues of Christ and His Church – surrounded by His Apostles, Saints, Martyrs and Confessors, in the middle of which, in the central *trumeau* (pier or pillar), is Christ as the Teacher, right hand upraised, left hand offering the Scriptures.

Inside

The immediate prospect on entering, particularly on a bright day, is encountering the seeming gloom. This always used to disappoint, until the realisation that a more brightly lit church inside would diminish the effect of the many and beautiful stained glass windows being illuminated by the daylight from outside. So, wait patiently for eyes to fully adjust before proceeding.

The nave claims to be the widest in France, and there is an uninterrupted view of some 120 metres straight down to the apse, with its high clerestory windows. The cathedral floor of ancient smooth-worn flags slopes down very gently back to the west door to enable the detritus of the many pilgrims of yesteryear, who often spent the night (or nights) sleeping in the cathedral, to be cleaned out.

Once you have orientated and start moving round, you will soon see that Chartres cathedral is an absolute feast of the most gorgeous display of stained glass, one hundred and sixty seven windows in total – roses, oculi and lancets – of many sizes and at many levels, showing over five thousand figures. As with the statuary, do not feel duty bound to try and get to grips with it all. There are very good and detailed guide books available in the cathedral shop which decodes it all – so just drift, and examine in detail those that catch your eye! Most of the glasswork dates back to the early 13th century, and all of it, amazingly, was painstakingly removed and stored in safety during the Second World War.

Windows

Of particular note are the earlier, 12th century lancets above the West portal – behind you as you go in – depicting the Tree of Jesse, the life of Our Lord, and the Passion. Above those is the West rose window, at just over twelve metres wide, showing scenes of the Last Judgement. But to me, it is the other two roses in the transept – North and South – that take the limelight, for here the advantage of the flying buttress is fully taken in enabling the profusion of glasswork.

The window of the 'Blue Virgin'.

The North rose, with its many contrasting shapes, including unusually, squares, is the one that intrigues. This window glorifies Our Lady surrounded by figures from the Old Testament: prophets in the circles, Kings of Judah in the squares. The South rose illustrates the Second Coming of the Lord.

The other window worth lingering over is the 'Blue Virgin', in the bay next to the South portal, opposite the start of the carved choir screen. This is one of the surviving 12th century St Fulbert windows, with Virgin and Child in a remarkably clear depiction mainly in deep blue, set against a dramatic background of ruby.

Chapels

One of the things that struck me on starting to wander round was the lack of the usual side chapels off the nave – there are some, but they are grouped round the ambulatory at the top end of the church. Here you will encounter a 16th century statue of Our Lady of the Pillar – one of two 'Black Madonna' statues in the cathedral – robed in rich vestments and surrounded by a blaze of devotional candles.

The other ambulatory chapels are that of the Blessed Sacrament, with a statue of St Thérèse of Lisieux, and one of the others housing the *Sancta Camisia*, in a glass fronted reliquary, supported by two kneeling angels. Dividing the ambulatory from the sanctuary is the magnificent, carved 16th century screen, with the sculptures depicting the lives of Jesus and Our Lady being added variously between the 16th and 18th centuries.

The Labyrinth

Back up to the area of the nave by the west door is the 13th century labyrinth, for which the cathedral is also well known, and one of the few surviving; it may be partially obscured by chairs placed over it. Labyrinths in churches were popular in the Middle Ages – symbolising one's meandering journey through life, tantalisingly getting close to the centre, only to be diverted away, until finally reaching that goal.

These labyrinths – reassuringly – never had any cul-de-sacs or dead-ends! It was said to be used as an aid to prayer and meditation, by those following its convoluted route. This labyrinth is a complex eleven circuit design, of four quadrants, representing the arms of the cross. The walking length is 861 feet; the diameter is 42 feet.

Crypt

The Crypt, claimed to be the third largest in the world, after St Peter's in Rome and Canterbury, is open at various times for a guided tour (in French). The Crypt dimensions partly explain why the cathedral is so expansive, as it was built over the Crypt. In the Crypt are a series of small chapels, the Well of Saint-Forts, round which Druid worship was centred, and down which two Christian martyrs were thrown by Norsemen in 858 during the siege of Chartres. Beyond the well is a large chapel which houses the second *Vierge Noire* of the cathedral – Notre Dame Sous Terre – Our Lady of the Crypt. It is the third replacement statue since before the French Revolution.

This beautiful cathedral is a memorable place in every way, of which I am sure any amount of visits will not satiate one's appetite for more!

PONTMAIN

"Mary teaches us how to pray...Mary never tires of asking the children to pray."

Pope Paul VI

If there is a jewel in the crown of the Shrines of France it has got to be Pontmain. I knew absolutely nothing about this Marian apparition site until my pilgrim travels took me there. It is just south off the Cherbourg peninsula, some 45 miles north east of Rennes, off the A84/E3; it is also not far from Mont

St Michel. If you have the chance on your travels passing nearby, take it – the basilica is stunning!

It would have been one of those typical sleepy French 'crossroads' rural villages had it not been for the apparition of Our Lady in 1871, thus taking it from its previous anonymity to the status of major pilgrim venue. The village therefore largely consists of the churches and buildings reflecting that event, and is geared to welcoming the pilgrims, but it does it gently and charmingly, and seemingly is not overwhelmed.

Apparition of Our Lady

The happenings at Pontmain need to be set in context. January 1871 saw France at the height of the Franco-Prussian War and in a desperate state – two thirds of France had been overrun, and the Germans were about to attack the town of Laval, not far from Pontmain. Many of the local young men had been conscripted into the French Army – Pontmain was praying for their safety, and for peace.

On a clear cold, snowy January winter's night Our Lady appeared in apparition just above the village, initially to two young brothers of the Barbadette family working in their barn, later joined by two young girls from the school, who also witnessed the apparition. With the excitement of the children growing, villagers started gathering, along with the parish priest Fr

Guérin, and the school teacher Sr Vitaline. Our Lady was very distinctly dressed with an unusual, plain turban-style crown with veil, and a full-length dark blue, star-spangled robe – a vesture in complete contrast to her other appearances, before or since.

The apparition, lasting some three hours, proceeded and developed over four distinct phases, all very detailed and charged with symbology – see Donal Foley's CTS booklet *'Apparitions of Mary'* for its historical and scriptural connotations. The villagers, although they could see nothing other than three stars – that were not of the night sky – in the area, all prayed fervently, led by Fr Guérin. Our Lady was silent, but her gestures of joy and sorrow at the various stages of the apparition were apparent.

The central theme of the apparition was the revealing of a message on a scroll that appeared under Our Lady – being excitedly spelt out, individually, by the young seers:

OH! DO PRAY MY CHILDREN GOD WILL ANSWER YOU VERY SOON ●
MY SON LETS HIS HEART BE TOUCHED

The children were very insistent about the exact composition of the letters – in capitals, the one large full stop, and the underlining of the last sentence – all of which adds authenticity to what they saw.

The next day, inexplicably, the German advance on Laval halted. It has been reported that Prussians in the front line saw an appearance of the Madonna over a distant village – some fleeing in fear. Ten days later the armistice was signed between France and Germany. The dry bones of history may not give any direct link between the apparition and the cessation of hostilities, but the people of Pontmain and surrounding area certainly knew why – maybe the rest of France did too. In answer to their prayers, the young men of Pontmain came home safe from the war, and peace was declared.

After the necessary canonical investigations the local bishop issued his judgement that the apparition could be held as authentic and that Our Lady of Prayer of Pontmain could be given due veneration. Pope Pius XI endorsed the bishop's approval to universal recognition by the Church. The three words that sum up the Pontmain apparition are: Peace, Hope, Prayer.

Basilica of Our Lady of Prayer

The basilica is the jewel. Construction was started soon after the apparition in 1873, being consecrated in 1900. It has a classic look, being built in Gothic style – a combination of strength and delicacy – but as you will see when you go inside, it also has a very modern feel to it. The front façade has a strong, intricate

Pontmain - casscades of light.

symmetry, with its graceful, free standing flanking towers and their needle-point spires. In the parvis, in front of the basilica, is the statue of Our Lady of Pontmain, as she appeared, holding the blood-red Crucifix, marking the spot above which the apparition took place.

When you enter, just be prepared to be overwhelmed by cascades of light pouring in through the abstract stained glass – particularly on a sunny day. For me, the first and enduring feature of this church is the huge expanse devoted to the windows – one of those rare, jaw-dropping 'wow!' moments. The effect is astonishing – the interior of the basilica is bathed in an ethereal, predominantly blue-shaded light, with splashes of red – the apparition colours.

As you walk down the smooth, soft pink-shaded stone flooring of the nave, you will notice the fine fluted columns reaching high up to the arched ceiling, and the more delicate arches into the side naves and side chapels, with the contrasting rough exposed stonework at the lower levels all round the church. The simple granite altar sits at the front of the sanctuary; the lower level of the apse displays soft, colourful, abstract images centred by the prominent Pontmain blood-red Crucifix. The arched windows above show predominantly the apparitions of Pontmain, Lourdes and la Salette.

The right hand apsidal side chapel is the Blessed Sacrament chapel, with a bold, modern tabernacle set into the wall. The left hand chapel is the Lady Chapel, with a striking white marble statue of Our Lady of Pontmain, contrasted only by the vivid red Crucifix and her golden crown. It is usually ablaze with candles and swamped by flowers! Both chapels have very delicate, miniature stained glass windows, contrasting effectively in size and colour with the main windows. The detail of the large, transept windows above each side chapel are worth studying for their rich symbolism in portraying, on the left, the Litany of Our Lady, and on the right, the Litany of the Sacred Heart.

As you turn to go out, you will see the enormous rose window at the back, with the lustrous organ pipes ranked beneath it. You may also notice the particularly striking Stations of the Cross – blue and white glazed and enamelled medallions, set in a cross with semi precious stones. Exiting out into the narthex, on your left is the glassed-in chapel of light, with the floor-to-ceiling mosaic of the apparition. It is open all the time for pilgrims to come in and light their candles in prayer.

Other Places in Pontmain

La Grange: Just diagonally opposite the basilica is the barn (La Grange) in which the Barbadette family were working when Our Lady appeared in the sky outside – easily recognised by the 3-D image of Our Lady of Pontmain neatly carved out of the roof thatch. Just walk inside and view the static display of the event, or for a couple of coins, you can initiate a charming, short sound (in French) and light presentation of the apparition sequence.

Parish Church: The 14th century parish church of SS Simon and Jude is another little jewel. This neat, solid, rough-stone church sits at a jaunty angle to the street, facing across to the basilica. As you go in, the first thing you will notice is its unusual elliptical barrelled wooden-planked ceiling of star spangled blue, running the full length of the church and showing the four phases of the apparition; it was painted in 1860. The flat faced apse with its temple-like arrangement of altar and statuary, predominantly in gold, is pleasing to the eye – the tabernacle a plain cylinder of brushed gold. On the right, the Blessed Sacrament chapel; on the left the Lady Chapel, with a picture of the parish priest at the time of the apparitions, Fr Michel Guérin, on display.

Chapel of the Oblates of Mary Immaculate: The Pontmain Sanctuary is run by the Oblates of Mary Immaculate, and their complex of buildings is at the other end, and beyond the basilica. Their chapel is open and welcomes pilgrims. It is a modern chapel, described architecturally as 'igloo', or 'African hut' shaped. Its unusually shaped interior is accentuated by the deep arches which house the long, narrow abstract stained glass windows at the top level, with beneath them at floor level, wide, arched windows in 'chunky' stained glass of muted colours, showing scenes from the Old and New Testament. The apse is also unusual with its low-lying, half egg-shaped shallow recessed arches, with their Middle Eastern style patterns depicting the Sacred Heart. The apse wall is plain, set off by the very effective stained glass silhouette of Christ in His Glory, set directly into the wall. A handsome, conventional exterior rather belies what is inside – a rather curious building, well worth having a look at. There are extensive gardens here in which you can wander peacefully.

Pastoral Centre: The Pastoral Centre for the Sanctuary is over the road from the side of the basilica at No 3. The helpful and obliging staff will provide you with basic information for your visit, and you can view a video of the apparition events, in English. Very reasonable pilgrim accommodation is available here. There is a pilgrim bookshop in the same street.

The Way of Life: Just on the outskirts of the village there is a delightful woodland walk with fourteen meditation points, similar to, but not exactly matching, the Stations of the Cross. Each station is mounted on a cross, and each scene is shown by a simple hand painted picture, the whole surrounded by a carefully tended and colourful flower bed. The large – by now familiar – blood red Crucifix of Pontmain, features. A peaceful place in which to wander and contemplate.

SAINT-LAURENT-SUR-SÈVRE

"Thanks to St Louis of Montfort, I came to understand that true devotion to the Mother of God is actually Christocentric, indeed it is very profoundly rooted in the Mystery of the Blessed Trinity, and the mysteries of the Incarnation and Redemption."

Pope John Paul II

The Village of St Laurent

This large village in the Vendée gives extraordinary testament to the legacy of St Louis-Mary Grignion de Montfort, with the spires of two major churches dominating the skyline, the large school nearby, and the considerable complex of buildings housing the three religious orders inspired by him, known as the Montfortian Family: The Daughters of Wisdom, the Montfortian Missionaries, and the Brothers of St Gabriel. From this small village radiates the reputation of one of the great saints of the Rosary, deeply devoted to Our Lady, and the ongoing ministry of these organisations, that today serve the world-wide Church.

St Laurent is about seven miles south of the bustling, modern town of Cholet, off the A87 and N149, straddling the meandering Sèvre Nantaise river. It does not have a great deal to offer in terms of the general tourist or traveller, devoting itself entirely to the pilgrim. But it is a tranquil, rural spot, off the beaten track, and offering a spiritual treasure chest, as well as exposing this great man's endeavours. All the pilgrim places are within a short walk of each other.

St Louis-Mary Grignion de Montfort

"If we do not risk anything for God we will never do anything great for Him"

St Louis de Montfort

Louis was born in Brittany, in 1673. He knew at an early stage in his life that he was called to the priesthood. He also had an early affinity for serving the poor, immediately giving away his new clothes, bought to equip him for his studies in Paris, to a beggar. After hardships, illness and living in extreme poverty, he was ordained in 1700, aged twenty seven. It was also clear that he had a cutting intellect, deep spirituality and a great gift for preaching.

He set about his mission of serving the poor and spreading the gospel throughout Brittany. He was a controversial figure at the time, with his zeal, enthusiasm, dedication, and sometimes unorthodox ways of preaching, and blunt opinions proving an irritant to the more conventionally minded of his religious colleagues. But the people loved him for his sincerity, his caring attitude, and his daring. He was often asked to move on by local bishops, eventually becoming so desperate for affirmation of his mission that he walked to Rome for an audience with the Pope. Clement XI was obviously moved by this ardent young man, sending him back to France as an Apostolic Missionary – but with the proviso of not upsetting the bishops!

He spent the rest of his life as a mendicant, preaching missions to parishes, always walking to his destinations, travelling down as far as la Rochelle, south of Nantes. He was always poor, sparing his own needs, becoming known affectionately as the 'vagabond priest'. During this period he also took time out to write extensively, not only major treatises on Our Lady, but also many poems and hymns. Amazingly, it was only after a century later that these writings, hidden away during the French Revolution, were discovered quite by chance (as he had prophesied) and published, and are now in wide and acclaimed use today.

His work is being considered with a view to declaring him a Doctor of the Church. He also wrote the Rules for the Daughters of Wisdom, an order co-founded with Marie-Louise Trichet and Catherine Brunet, whom he met in his early years working in a hospital for the poor in Poitiers. For his priests serving in the missions, he wrote Rules, which are the basis for the Company of Mary (the Montfortian Missionaries).

After his many years of non-stop ministry, Louis, weakened by exhaustion and illness – there were even mutterings of a plot to poison him – died in St Laurent in 1716, aged 43, whilst giving a mission. Although only known regionally for a very long time, it was his writings that subsequently not only spoke to the people, but also had a profound effect on some modern Popes – Pope John Paul II being one, whose personal motto *'Totus tuus'* was inspired by St Louis's self-dedication and consecration to Our Lady.

Louis de Montfort was canonised by Pope Pius XII in 1947, and his feast day is celebrated on 28th April.

One of the two proven miracles required to support St Louis's canonisation was the complete cure of an English nun of the Daughters of Wisdom in Romsey, Hampshire, so gravely ill that the doctor arrived on his next visit with her death certificate already filled in! Pope John Paul visited St Laurent in 1996, praying before the tombs of St Louis and Blessed Mary-Louise Trichet. Full details of his life can be found in the CTS booklet *'Louis Marie de Montfort'*. St Louis is the patron saint of the Legion of Mary.

You can usually recognise statues of St Louis – hair curling over his forehead, long aquiline nose, set in a strong determined face, always with his accompanying motifs – a large crucifix, usually held aloft, and a prominent rosary at his waist.

"Virgin, faithful pure, God's chosen Mother, / Fill me with a measure of your faith; / That way Wisdom will come to me / And all his attendant treasures."

St Louis de Montfort

Basilica of Saint Louis-Marie de Montfort

This fetching Romanesque-Byzantine style basilica, replacing the original 11th century church on this site, was started in 1889, built in stages, and was finally completed in 1949. It is fronted by a narrow plaza, surrounded by a few village shops, including a

St Louis-Mary Grignion de Montfort.

pilgrim bookshop. Two slender, three-sided towers with ovoid domes flank the symmetrical front façade, with the imposing main bell tower being offset at the end of the left transept.

It is relatively light inside, the centre nave being supported by white limestone columns, reaching up to a plain, light, vaulted ceiling. The focal point, in the left transept, is the raised, black marble tombs of St Louis and Blessed Marie-Louise of Jesus, arranged side by side, under a white sculpted ciborium-styled canopy, surmounted by angels and supported by contrasting dark green marble pillars.

The first side chapel on the left is dedicated to Our Lady, and in which the Blessed Sacrament resides. The statue of Our Lady is from the original church, in front of which St Louis regularly prayed. The last side chapel on the left is dedicated to St Louis, a statue of whom fittingly looks out over his tomb, opposite. The side chapels on the right of the sanctuary are dedicated to St Joseph and St Laurent.

The windows in the transept and sanctuary show the Mysteries of the Rosary, and down the nave, scenes from St Louis's life. Rosary beads form a continuous thread round the transept and sanctuary, just under the windows. The crypt, below, is normally locked, but in a quiet moment, the person attending the reception desk in the basilica may open it for you.

Blessed Marie-Louise of Jesus

Marie-Louise Trichet was born in Poitiers in 1684, eleven years after St Louis. In meeting Louis, when she was aged seventeen, she expressed her desire for the religious life. He sent her to work in Poitiers hospital for the poor, where he was chaplain. Thus started a long association, where Marie devoted her life to ministering to the poor and the sick. Before leaving Poitiers in 1703, Louis formalised Marie's status by giving her the Rules of the Daughters of Wisdom, and endowing her with the religious habit of the order – she was the first Daughter of Wisdom.

During his subsequent travels he kept in touch with her and encouraged her ministry and fledgling Order. Encouraged by the Bishop of La Rochelle, and under Louis's direction, Marie and her companion Catherine Brunet established a successful free school there in 1715, thus focusing another aspect of the apostolic mission of the Daughters of Wisdom.

After Louis died in 1716, Marie had to assume full responsibility of the Order, moving to St Laurent and establishing the Mother House. They lived and worked in abject poverty, but gradually the Order grew, establishing in her lifetime thirty-six other houses round France, devoted to tending the poor and the sick.

She died in 1759, after a fall and an illness, on the same day and same place that Louis had died exactly forty three years earlier. She was beatified by Pope John Paul II in 1993.

Mother House of the Daughters of Wisdom
(La Sagesse)

Pilgrims are welcome to visit the Mother House, just round the corner from the basilica: check in at the small reception gate house. There is much to see inside – all tastefully and thoughtfully presented, and with a simple charm and homely air about it all.

You may visit the Founder's Chapel, view a display of St Louis' writings and artefacts, and off the enclosed cloister garden go into the former room of the travellers' inn, where St Louis died – now his Oratory. Inside is an ornate glass fronted case in which lies a full-sized recumbent effigy of St Louis, fully garbed, lifting the statue of Our Lady to his lips, and in his other hand his crucifix blessed by Clement XI. Inscribed on the wall above – his simple motto – 'God Alone'.

Down one side of the main cloister is a display of the countries of the world where the Sisters serve – some twenty-three, including Great Britain and Ireland in which there are eleven houses. Opportunities for men to stay in retreat in the Abbey, individually or in small groups are available. There are retreat facilities for mixed groups in other nearby properties owned by the abbey.

Chapel of Wisdom

In complete contrast to the basilica is this elegant, neo-Gothic church, built between 1862 and 1869 as the convent chapel, with its distinctive, delicate needle point spire reaching high. 'Chapel' may be a bit of a misnomer, because it is actually a sizeable church – the nave being some 65 metres long. Although it can be reached by walking all the way round the outside and through its grounds, you can also get to it through the Mother House – although directions may be required!

Inside it is beautiful, with its finely worked pillars, arches, trellises and galleries; its elaborate, ornately carved pulpit is said to weigh forty-five tons! The whole is complemented by exquisite stained glass windows, in their delicate Gothic arches, of which the main theme in the nave is the Beatitudes.

Montfortian Missionaries

Almost opposite the entrance to La Sagesse is the entrance leading you into the grounds, and Mother House, of the Company of Mary – the Montfortian Missionaries. Although he had written the Rules for the Company of Mary, there was no formal membership of the Order during his lifetime. It was only after his untimely death that the priests engaged in his missions formally instituted the Order, in which today nearly a thousand priests and brothers serve the Church in some thirty-one countries round the world; there are four houses in England.

Of interest here is their lovely small chapel to Our Lady of the Rosary. It was built in 1852/3 in the Romanesque style. Inside, it is a plain church, the focus being the tabernacle, with its illuminated mosaic door. On one side, a large crucifix, on the other, opposite, a small Madonna and Child, and St Louis – crucifix held high – urging people onwards. On a practical note, toilets are also available by the entrance to the complex.

The Brothers of St Gabriel

Although its roots took hold in the schools for the poor set up during and after St Louis's death, it was not until after the French Revolution in 1835 that this Order was formally re-organised with its specific apostolate of teaching, particularly disadvantaged and handicapped children. The organisation therefore caters to the educational needs of not only children and youth in normal academic schools, but also imparts technical education, education of the deaf, the dumb and the blind, the physically and mentally handicapped, and engaging in social work for marginalised youngsters. Recent statistics show that the congregation has a hundred and seventy schools and colleges round the world.

Their House is at Maison Supiot, next to the school, and next door to that is the Montfortian Gabrielist Centre, which has information and an exhibition on the activities of the community. The school itself caters for about two thousand pupils, and the school chapel, St Gabriel, is normally available to visitors.

In summing up the ethos and spirit of the Montfortian Family:

> *"To God alone, by Christ in Wisdom, in the Spirit, in communion with Mary, for the reign of God".*

TOURS

> *"No one ever saw him enraged, or excited, or lamenting, or laughing; he was always one and the same: displaying a kind of heavenly happiness in his countenance, he seemed to have passed the ordinary limits of human nature. Never was there any word on his lips but Christ, and never was there a feeling in his heart except piety, peace, and tender mercy."*

Sulpitius Serverus, St Martin of Tours's biographer

Although Tours is not especially known as a major international pilgrim destination, it does hold the memory of one of France's most loved and highly regarded saints – St Martin of Tours. It was here also that devotion to the Holy Face of Jesus was started by a Carmelite nun, Sister Marie of St Peter in 1843, after seeing a vision. At about the same time, nightly adoration of the Blessed Sacrament was started by Venerable Leo Dupont – the 'Holy Man of Tours' – from whence this devotion, and that of the Holy Face, spread throughout France. The victory of the Battle of Tours in 732 is regarded as a crucial stage in turning back invading Islamic forces; this in turn, laid the foundation of the Carolingian Empire.

The town of Tours sits between two rivers – the Loire to the north, and the Cher to the south. With its several attractive parks, it is known as the 'Garden of France'. Despite severe damage during World War II, much of its original mediaeval district – *Le Vieux Tours* – remains intact, with its appealing half-timbered buildings.

Saint Martin of Tours

Martin, named after the god of war – Mars – was born in about 316, the son of a tribune in the Roman army. At the early age of ten, and against the wishes of his parents, he became a catechumen and candidate for baptism. Aged fifteen, and following the military tradition of his family, he joined the Roman army, and was stationed in what is now Amiens. It was here that the famous episode of the cloak took place – seeing a poorly clad, shivering beggar, he cut his cloak in half, giving one half to the beggar. That night he had a dream of Jesus, wearing his half cloak, and saying to him, "Here is Martin the Roman soldier, who is not baptised; he has clad me". Greatly affirmed in his faith, he was baptised, aged eighteen.

Two years later, the day before the battle of Worms in 336, he declared, "I am a soldier of Christ. I cannot fight". Accused of cowardice, he offered to lead the troops into battle, unarmed. The battle never took place, but on the basis of his belief and his assertion of courage, he was released from military service. In fulfilling his new vocation, Martin headed for Tours, becoming a disciple of Hilary of Poitiers. When Hilary was forced into exile, Martin ranged through Italy, living in part, an eremitical life. With the return of Hilary to his see in 361, Martin rejoined him, founding an abbey in the remote location of Ligugé, from where he evangelised widely throughout the country districts of Gaul.

His desire for solitude and his lonely missions, was brought to an abrupt end, when by popular acclamation Martin was obliged to become the third Bishop of Tours in 371. Not wanting to change his simple lifestyle, he moved a short distance from Tours, founding another monastery, Marmoutier. From here he continued to discharge his episcopal duties, travelling throughout his diocese, educating and evangelising, and establishing in effect a rudimentary parochial system.

On returning from a visit to Rome, Martin died, aged 81 in 397. His body was taken to Tours, initially to a chapel, and later, in 470, to the first basilica built to his memory. Many miracles were attributed to him during his lifetime, and to his intercession since his death. He was very popular during the Middle Ages, many churches round the world being named after him, including St Martin-in-the-Fields in Trafalgar Square, and what is claimed to be the biggest church in Asia, at Taal in the Philippines. He is one of the patron saints of France, and the patron saint of soldiers and beggars. His feast day is on the 11th of November.

Pilgrim places in Tours

Basilica of St Martin of Tours: As with many Christian sites of the 4th century, the churches placed here have a tumultuous past. The 5th century basilica

Basilica of St Martin of Tours.

burned down in 988; another was built in 1014, but
burned down in 1230. A large Romanesque basilica
was built in the 13th century, which became a focal
national pilgrim place, as well as a stop-off point for
pilgrims on their way to Santiago. In 1562 the
Huguenots sacked the church, destroying the tomb
and relics of St Martin. The church was subsequently
restored, but during the French Revolution it was
destroyed, leaving only the two towers that still stand
today. In ensuring that another church would not be
placed on that site, the municipality of the time built
two streets through it. In1860 the site was excavated,
and a few remaining fragments were discovered. The
present, smaller basilica, designed in neo-Byzantine
style, was built between 1886 and 1924, fittingly over
the spot where St Martin's tomb lay. St Martin's relics
and shrine are in the crypt, on the walls of which are
carved many votive prayers of his followers.

St Gatien's Cathedral: This dizzyingly ornate and
intricate cathedral, dedicated to its first bishop, had a
prolonged construction – starting in the 12th century,
and finally reaching completion at the beginning of
the 16th century. This inevitably saw an assortment of
styles being incorporated – principally a mix of
Romanesque and Gothic, with a touch of
Renaissance! Inside it is the epitome of elegance, and

has some fine 14th century stained glass windows, particularly round the sanctuary, and including a fine rose window in the north transept. One of the windows depicts St Martin's ordination as bishop – in which he looks distinctly reluctant!

SOLESMES

The **Benedictine Abbey of St Peter's** is at Solesmes, near the town of Sablé-sur-Sarthe, some 60 kms south west of Le Mans, off the A11/E501. A Benedictine priory was established here in 1010, which apart from the ravages of the Hundred Years War, had an uneventful history until it was dispersed in 1791 during the French Revolution. In 1831 the remaining run-down buildings of the abbey were due for demolition for want of a buyer. An enterprising and locally born priest, Prosper Guéranger, had the desire and the vision to revive monastic life in France, and with some colleague priests, and against all odds, purchased the property and re-established a Benedictine community.

The community flourished, receiving Papal approval in 1837, and was instituted as the Benedictine Congregation of France, a worthy successor to the Cluny community. The monks were expelled during the upheavals of the Third Republic,

Benedictine Abbey of St Peter's.

going into exile in 1901 to the Isle of Wight, where they built Quarr Abbey, which still flourishes today as a Solesmes foundation. The community returned to Solesmes in 1922. Solesmes is noted for its devotion to the liturgy and Gregorian plainchant, and has founded 28 monasteries in France and abroad.

The solid, blunt abbey complex overlooks the River Sarthe. On entering the abbey church you will be struck by the slender, long medieval nave, which extends on into the monks' choir, added in the 19th century. What is particularly striking, and worthy of close examination, is the statuary in the two transepts. The southern (right hand) transept depicts, in a 15th century ensemble, the Passion and a very dramatic tableau of the entombment of Jesus. The northern transept, with over a hundred carved Renaissance figures, is dedicated to Our Lady. Unusually for a western church, the lower tableau, which mirrors the entombment scene in the other transept, features the Dormition of Our Lady, in which one's eyes and soul are immediately drawn to the beautiful, serene and tranquil expression on Our Lady's face.

The monks live an enclosed life within the cloister, but the abbey church is open to the public, and they may participate in the Daily Office of the community. There is a bookshop.

L'ÎLE BOUCHARD

"Tell the little children to pray for France, for her need is great."

Our Lady of Prayer, L'Île Bouchard

The Apparitions of Our Lady of Prayer

The village of L'Île Bouchard is about 25 miles south of Tours to the west of the A10/E5. It is the site of the most recent apparition (1947) reported, and authenticated, in France. Four village children had a series of apparitions in the village church – St Gilles – over a period of seven days. Our Lady's message was one of prayer and sacrifice in order to address national crises.

The apparitions were accompanied by a minor miracle, when one of the young seer's poor eyesight was completely cured. The final apparition was concluded – as Our Lady promised the young seers, and witnessed by the large crowd – with an inexplicable appearance, in physical terms, of a spreading and radiating shaft of sunlight that appeared in the church on that dull winter's day. The week of the apparitions was also the week that the Communist inspired nationwide strike collapsed.

Shrine of Our Lady of Prayer.

Soon after the apparitions, a grotto with Our Lady and the angel Gabriel, who attended her in the apparitions, was constructed in the church – as requested by Our Lady. Progress for ecclesiastical approval was slow, reportedly hindered by a succession of parish priests who were resistant to the apparitions. However, momentum was regained in 2001, when the Bishop of Tours authorised veneration of Our Lady of Prayer at St Gilles, and permitted organised pilgrimages to be made there.

Shrine of Our Lady of Prayer

The Shrine of Our Lady of Prayer is situated in the humble parish church of St Gilles, with its rough-faced, weathered, exterior limestone blockwork, and blunt, square tower. Inside is the simple and charming white-statued tableau depicting the apparition: Our Lady, with her long tresses well below her waist – as described by the seers – her outstretched hand offering a crucifix, a rosary suspended from her wrist. The angel Gabriel kneels in attendance, proffering a gilded lily, the whole scene surrounded by a golden cave.

It is a simple, charming place – a far cry from the major apparition sites such as Lourdes and Pontmain – but one with a message just as powerful. The New Movement Emmanuel Community are engaged here in the mission of Our Lady of Prayer, through events, pilgrimages and retreats at the parish, and at their nearby house at Chezelles.

PELLEVOISIN

The small village of Pellevoisin is about 60 miles south east of Tours, just south of the D943. It was at this village that a domestic worker, Estelle Faguette, had fifteen apparitions of Our Lady during 1876. The initial apparitions led up to a miraculous cure from her death-bed illness of tuberculosis. The remainder were concerned mainly with promoting the Scapular of the Sacred Heart. Whilst the apparitions as such were never approved by the local bishop or the Church, there have been 'secondary levels' of approval, such as Pope Leo XIII supporting the promotion of the Scapular of the Sacred Heart, and the Bishop of Bourges approving public veneration of Our Lady of Pellevoisin and leading the annual pilgrimage. A Theological Commission of Enquiry did, however, adjudge that her healing was miraculous (Estelle lived on another fifty years after her cure), and that with her healing, "God wished to appeal to our faith and bring credibility to a message".

Chapel of Our Lady of Mercy.

Sanctuary of Our Lady of Mercy in Pellevoisin, where pilgrims head for, contains the Chapel of Apparitions – the converted bedroom where Estelle had her apparitions. There is a reception area, small bookshop and simple lodging facilities, all based round the cloistered convent of the Sisters of Saint John. It is very low key and tranquil; for those who really want somewhere off the beaten track, this is the place.

ÎLE DE FRANCE
☙ PARIS ☙

Paris

Paris: bustling, vibrant, stylish – at times haughty, at times down at heel – but offering every imaginable attraction of any major city, and thus drawing millions of visitors every year. As part of their visit, some may come with an element of pilgrim intent, maybe wishing to seek out a particular devotion to which they are drawn, or others just to marvel more generally at some of the great Christian sites of the world as part of their overall 'Paris experience'. Of these great marvels, there are the imposing, solid Cathedral, where the simple descriptor **'Notre Dame'** will suffice, and the iconic Basilica of the **Sacré-Coeur of Montmartre**.

For those seeking out a specific devotion or favourite Saint, there are the Shrines of **St Vincent de Paul**; **St Catherine Labouré** and **St Louise de Marillac** at the Chapel of **Our Lady of the Miraculous Medal** (rue du Bac); and two very contrasting and special churches that I have indulged myself in selecting for you to consider: the quite extraordinary church of **La Madeleine**, and **St Augustine's** church, which has a strong association with **Blessed Charles de Foucauld**.

NOTRE DAME

"...a vast symphony in stone..."

Victor Hugo

First impressions

Notre Dame has got to be one of the most magnificent buildings in Christendom. Whether from afar or close-up, and from all angles, it presents a dizzying combination of strength, delicacy and intricacy – and sheer size. The sturdy, blunt towers and front façade, with its intricate detailing, could not be more of a contrast with the seemingly fragile needlepoint central spire reaching high, and the glorious, soaring, flying buttresses and mini-steeples, when viewed from the side or rear. Similarly, the vastness of the soaring interior, contrasting with the rich detail found in every nook and cranny, could prove overwhelming.

Two practical matters: some thirteen million people are claimed to visit the cathedral every year, so the large and somewhat noisy crowds and tours progressing round and through could prove to be an irritant, and, secondly, the initially gloomy interior when entering. Presented with all this – and wanting to get maximum benefit from my visit – I employ

Notre Dame.

well tried tactics: make a conscious effort (and keep making it!) to completely ignore and filter out the hubbub and crowds; on entering stay still for a while – to orientate, receive first impressions, and let the eyes adjust to the light level. And lastly, use the excellent brochure to conduct yourself systematically around at your own pace, making the effort not to get overwhelmed by the detail – thinking that you must look at absolutely everything – but just concentrate on and admire those aspects that particularly catch your eye or imagination.

History

The Île de la Cité is an obvious central point for the establishment of habitation in and around this strategic river, and so it has been for Paris – the city growing in ever increasing circles out from the island – and in many ways it is still the centre and heart of the city. There is evidence of pagan worship on this site, excavations having uncovered Gallic and Roman altars. The current cathedral is the fourth church to occupy the island. It is built principally in a grand Gothic style, with the then newly-discovered use of the flying buttress being fully maximised to free up more wall space for windows.

The cathedral has continued to develop and evolve over many centuries. The principal work was the construction of the sanctuary and the mighty nave, narthex and west façade between 1163 and 1220. Henry VI was crowned King of France here on 16th December 1431. During the French Revolution its treasures were pillaged, much of the interior was vandalised, and the building used as a warehouse for food. Extensive restoration was started in 1845, lasting twenty-three years to regain its former glory, and other, more recent restoration started in 1991, is ongoing.

Inside

Suffice to say in a book of this scope, I can give just a few impressions and memorable instances. In your explorations, you may notice the many side chapels down each side of the nave and round the apse, there are, in fact, twenty-five. The axial chapel right up at the head of the ambulatory is the Lady Chapel – Our Lady of Seven Sorrows, which is also the Blessed Sacrament Chapel, and is normally kept free from the 'viewing circuit', leaving it relatively quiet for prayer and reflection. Although you probably will not spot them all, there are thirty-seven major statues and representations of Our Lady round the cathedral.

As you start your tour, you will notice to your right, at the start of the nave, and above a blaze of votive candles, the huge bronze crucifix presented by Napoleon III. The massive organ, when you turn rearwards and look up to see its pipes ranked below the west rose window, is one of the largest in the world, with 113 stops and 7800 pipes.

As you walk on down the nave, you will notice on each side the substantial galleries ranged above. On reaching the transept, the huge rose windows will come into view; both in such immense detail as to give initially only impressions of size, complexity and colour, and requiring time if you wish to decipher them in any detail. The left window depicts the characters of the Old Testament, surrounding Madonna and Child, and, on the right, the emphasis is on the New Testament.

Sanctuary and screens

Butting in to the transept is the large, stepped, marble podium bearing the altar – quite a small, modern, gleaming, brushed bronze arrangement, showing in abstract outline, major prophets of the Old Testament and the Evangelists of the New. The choir, behind, is flanked by the solid, wooden choir stalls, burnished to a rich gleam by the passage of time, with above them, large, intricately carved panels showing various scenes involving Our Lady. At the head of the sanctuary is a dramatic composition of the Pietà, set beneath an empty golden cross, with on each side, Louis XIII and XIV paying homage. Encircling the whole group are six angels in bronze, each holding an instrument of the Passion.

One of the features that catches most attention are the extensive, carved and polychromed wooden screens separating ambulatory from choir. On the north side (left) the sequence portrays many incidents in the life of Jesus, including the Visitation, and twelve other composite scenes, leading to His Passion. The colours are vivid – recreating what they, and other statues throughout the church, would have looked like in the Middle Ages. Each scene stands out from a lustrous, gold embossed and patterned background. The southern screens show nine scenes in which Jesus appeared after the Resurrection. Much fine detail here, which may tempt you to linger!

Treasury

Off to the right of the sanctuary area is the Treasury, a modern addition to the cathedral, built in the middle of the 19th century. One can only imagine what was stored in the Cathedral in previous ages, as it has been subject to pillage and theft during those times of anti-religion. There are some precious and superb objects and artifacts on view. Not on direct view, and the most precious, is the reputed Crown of Thorns, whose provenance can be taken back to the 4th century, but not earlier. It was brought to France by Saint Louis in the mid 13th century. It is only brought to display for veneration on the first Friday of each month and on Fridays during Lent.

Outside

If you are feeling energetic, you can tackle the 422 steps up the towers, taking you diagonally upwards across the front façade, and rewarding your efforts with spectacular views across Paris from the top. The towers are managed separately by the Centre for National Monuments, and there is an entrance charge. The entrance is on the outside, into the left hand tower.

The archaeological crypt, displaying artifacts and elements from previous churches and buildings on this site, is under the cathedral parvis, entry being gained by staircases opposite the cathedral, near the Police Headquarters. The crypt is managed separately by Musée Carnavalet, and there is an entrance charge.

Having an idea of the vastness of what lay inside, I had abandoned my normal practice of wandering round the exterior before going in to get a feel for the whole, as I knew this in itself would be a lengthy undertaking! So I did this afterwards, mainly as a relaxation to clear my mind, and generally just admire the cathedral in its entirety. However, for those particularly with an architectural or statuary interest, a feast still awaits! The front façade has three immense arched portals, each surrounded by a myriad of carved statues, with the middle portal portraying the Last Judgment. Above these three arches is the phalanx of the twenty-eight ancestors of Jesus, named in St Matthew's Gospel. There is a pleasant garden down the south side where you can wander, enjoying the detail. What I would recommend, though, if you have the time, either on approach or departure, is to pause and view the cathedral in its setting, from the other side of the river.

Virgin Mary, at the heart of the City, We pray to you for this capital city. You, the Virgin, preserve the purity of its faith!

Virgin Mary, from the banks of the Seine, We pray to you for the country of France. O Mother, teach it to hope!

Virgin Mary, in this great Christian site, We pray to you for all the earth's people. You, full of grace, may they be one in Love.

Prayer of Pope John Paul II on his visit to Notre Dame in 1997

SACRÉ-COEUR OF MONTMARTRE

"...it is here the place of the martyrs, it is here where the Sacred Heart should reign where He can summon all to Him..."

Cardinal Guibert, Archbishop of Paris

Origins

This grand, yet delicate, gleaming white, Roman-Byzantine style Basilica, set in the heart and heights of Montmartre, dominates the Paris skyline – Montmartre so called after *Mons Martyrum*, the place of the martyring of St Denis, the first bishop of Paris, and his companions, who were beheaded here in the 3rd century.

The unique origins of the Basilica lie in the aftermath and sense of disgrace felt by the defeat of the French in the Franco-Prussian war of 1870, and also to make amends for the indignities inflicted on the Church in that period. Two prominent Catholic men vowed to erect a suitable church in reparation for 'national failings', and with the support of the Archbishop of Paris, secured the site through the French National Assembly for the purpose of expressing 'France repentant and devoted'.

Sacré-Coeur of Montmartre.

Building started in 1875, and was not without problems, political, financial and technical. Although the building was not yet complete, the date of 1st August 1885 is of great significance, it being the first time that the Blessed Sacrament was exposed in the Basilica – the start of Perpetual Adoration here. And so it has continued, without interruption, day and night, for the 125 years since: even the ravages of two World Wars did not stop the faithful from getting before the altar to adore the Lord. The Basilica was finally consecrated in 1919.

Outside

The terrace at the front, with its wide views of Paris laid out below, is invariably busy, and has a happy air – a buzzing crowd, sometimes being entertained by buskers, all seemingly in permanent party mode! But standing back from that, and looking up at the façade, will give a sense of the beauty of this graceful building, capped by the stone-scaled, ovoid cupola, topped by a slender, delicate-columned lantern, reaching even further upwards.

Although its execution is intricate and seemingly 'busy', there is a dignified and pleasing symmetry to the whole – the two flanking, smaller towers and cupolae, the balancing circles of the rose windows, the three uniformed entry archways. The mounted, green bronze statues of St Louis and St Joan of Arc, the only contrast to the acres of pale stone, stand sentinel at each side atop the porch. A large statue of the Sacred Heart of Jesus, hand raised in blessing, in the top pediment of the façade, welcomes all who enter.

Inside

Although in busy times there may be a bit of a procession tending to take you round the designated 'visitor route', it may well be worth peeling off straight away, and going into an area reserved for those who have come to pray, and after paying homage to Our Lord in the monstrance being held aloft by two golden angels above the high altar, to just quietly sit and take in the splendid interior in slow time.

The excellent brochure will give you a good detailed 'decode' of all that is before you, but you will no doubt be struck by the vast, brilliant, predominantly azure blue and vibrant gold apse mosaic of Jesus, arms stretched wide in acceptance, and revealing his Sacred Heart. The heavenly figures of Our Lady and St Michael the Archangel, each side, are gazing up, and kneeling in offering; diminutive figures of Pope Leo XIII and St Joan of Arc also kneel before Him. Around Him, at 'ground' level, the ranked figures of the Catholic Church (left) and France (right) give homage;

above Him, the Church of Heaven (left) and the
France of Heaven (right). Underneath there is a motto
in Latin: 'To the Most Sacred Heart of Jesus, France,
fervent, penitent and grateful'.

Walk round

Having taken in the general sense of it all, noting the
huge nave arches supported by their stepped columns,
and the fact that the whole nave is as wide as it is
long, it would be worth taking a slow walk round,
examining the detail. There are thirteen side chapels,
six round the nave, and seven apsidal chapels. Unlike
side chapels in some churches, which have an air of
neglect and disuse, all these are fresh, bright and
vivid, quite individual and beautifully crafted in their
own way, and all merit some examination.

Before you go round the ambulatory you can
examine the finer detail of the altar and sanctuary
area, surrounded by eleven slim, tall, elaborately be-
pillared arches, and also the dome, with its plain
cupola, and two galleries – one a galleried walkway,
the other letting in light through the twenty stained
glass windows. At the head of each nave, close to the
ambulatory, is on the left, a silver statue of the
Madonna and Child, and on the right, the Sacred
Heart. The axial chapel is an exquisite Lady chapel
dedicated to the Immaculate Heart. It is worth

lingering here, particularly noting the fine mosaic of the Assumption adorning the small cupola. Opposite this chapel is a copy of the sitting statue of St Peter, as found in St Peter's, Rome.

Above and below

Note the striking side chapel, back left as you head out, of St Michael the Archangel and St Joan of Arc. Outside once again, you can access the dome with a stiff, steep circular climb, but once up there, there are spectacular views right across Paris and beyond, enabling you quite readily to pick out all the famous landmarks, from all round the exterior gallery.

You can also get to the crypt from outside – and a visit is recommended. Like the side chapels, the crypt looks loved and used. It is spacious, with a wide ambulatory, and handsome, sturdy arches and plain vaulted ceiling. In the centre of the crypt is the Chapel of the Pietà with a dramatic statue of the Pietà; there is also an unusual full size bronze statue of the recumbent Christ in death, commemorating the priests and seminarians who gave their lives during the two World Wars. Seven side chapels are found round the ambulatory. Opposite the apsidal chapel dedicated to the Holy Family, is the Chapel of St Peter, over which altar is an imposing *papier mâché* statue of the Sacred

Heart matching that designed by Charles de Foucauld for his desert chapel of Beni Abbes.

Retreat House

The Basilica is served by the Benedictine Sisters of the Sacré-Coeur of Montmartre, who are responsible for maintaining the Perpetual Adoration. They also run a well kept retreat house next to the Basilica – *Maison d'Accueil Ephrem* – at which pilgrims are welcome to come and stay overnight or more. The only criteria is that you come as a pilgrim, and attend community events such as the evening meal, Mass and some liturgy. I felt very privileged in doing this, particularly getting up in the small hours and going into the vast, darkened, cavernous beauty of the now empty and hushed church, joining just those other few, kneeling before the Lord.

Sacré-Coeur is a major venue in Paris, so much so – as one of the Sisters told me with just the smallest hint of satisfaction – that numbers visiting topped those for the Eiffel Tower. Despite these huge numbers, there is always an air of hush and reverence inside, contrasting to other religious sites, such as Notre Dame, which one can only put down to an innate sense of reverence and awe from those who visit – regardless of their beliefs. Again, unlike other major religious venues, the Basilica is discreetly managed by the stewards. The whole experience is further highlighted if you can join the Sisters in any of their Liturgies, listening to their sharp, clear singing voices, accompanied by the zinging of a zither.

"Come to me, all you who labour and are overburdened, and I will give you rest. Shoulder my yoke and learn from me, for I am gentle and humble in heart, and you will find rest for your souls."

Mt 11:28,29

CHAPEL OF OUR LADY OF THE MIRACULOUS MEDAL

"Have a medal made according to this model. Everyone who wears it around their neck will receive great graces. For those who wear it with confidence there will be abundant graces."

Our Lady to St Catherine Labouré

The Chapel of Our Lady of the Miraculous Medal, sometimes commonly known simply by its 7th Arondissement street location as 'rue du Bac', is where Catherine Labouré, a twenty-four year old novice sister of the Daughters of Charity of St Vincent de Paul, experienced three apparitions of Our Lady in 1830, giving her the mission of establishing the now worldwide devotion to the Miraculous Medal. The chapel houses the reliquaries of St Catherine Labouré and also St Louise de Marillac, co-founder, with St Vincent de Paul, of the Daughters of Charity. The chapel is the convent chapel to the Daughters' Motherhouse at rue du Bac. The nearest Metro is Sèvres-Babylone, not Rue du Bac.

It is a lovely shrine to visit, not only visually, but principally to experience this holy place at which Our Lady appeared, soaking up the buzzing atmosphere outside in the narrow courtyard and shop, and joining the faithful – and those seeking – from all parts of the world, in the contemplative mood inside the chapel-shrine.

Saint Catherine Labouré

"I knew nothing. I was nothing. For this reason God picked me out".

St Catherine Labouré

Catherine Labouré was born to a farming family in 1806 in Burgundy, the eighth of ten surviving children. On her mother's death she adopted Our Lady, saying, "Now you will be my mother". Against some family opposition she achieved her desire of leading a religious life by joining the Daughters of

Charity in 1830 – the choice of order being inspired by a dream she had of St Vincent de Paul, the founder, urging her to care for the sick. She only recognised the figure in the dream when she saw St Vincent's statue on her first visit to the Daughters.

In three apparitions between July and December 1830, Our Lady showed her in some detail the medal that she wanted made for all to wear – today's Miraculous Medal – based on the main motif, "O Mary, conceived without sin, pray for us who have recourse to thee". This of course was well before the dogma of the Immaculate Conception was declared by Pius XI in 1854. In humility she recounted her experiences to her confessor, who, doubting their veracity, instructed her to remain silent.

Miraculous Medal

Eventually, after Catherine had left rue du Bac to work in the community's hospice in Reuilly, the priest went to the Archbishop, who immediately understood the significance of the message, and ordered the medal to be struck and distributed, stating, "There is no question here of pre-judging the nature of the vision or its circumstances. We are simply going to distribute a medal. The tree will be judged by its fruits". Shortly after distribution the fruits began to appear: miracles, healings and conversions associated with it were being reported. It soon acquired the cachet 'Miraculous'.

For over forty years Catherine served her community at Reuilly, and although rumours circulated about the identity of the visionary, they were never traced to Catherine – who kept resolutely silent. It was only nearing death, and feeling Our Lady's prompting, that she confided in her Superior, from whom the secret emerged. She died aged seventy in 1876. She was buried at Reuilly, where she was venerated until 1933, the year she was beatified, when her body, found to be incorrupt, was moved to rue du Bac. She was canonised in 1947 by Pope Pius XII, declaring her, "The saint who lived a dutiful life, and silent life!", giving her the title of the 'Silent Saint'.

In amongst the bustle of rue du Bac you might miss the entrance to the Chapel. There is no great spire or bulk to announce its presence – you won't know you are there until you see a small arch with the standard French blue address number plate designating it as number '140' – but Our Lady and the Child Jesus above the arch will certainly reassure you. In the long narrow courtyard – more like a small cul-de-sac – you will encounter the bustle of people examining the statues, bas reliefs and plaques up one side, or engaging in the shop and accueil on the other, leading up to the chapel. This of course, is the opportunity to purchase your Miraculous Medals – at source – for further distribution! There is usually no shortage of priests available to bless them for you.

The Chapel

You enter the Chapel to your right, at the end of the courtyard. Inside it is not large, but gives the impression of light and space. You will be immediately confronted with a series of statues, side chapels, altars, reliquaries – all ranked side by side in the sanctuary area. It may be worth just taking a seat before you wander and examine the detail, to sort what's what, using the very useful small brochure, or one of the postcards detailing the principal features. As you look around, also note the slender, octagonal pillars reaching up to the galleried side chapels above, with their delicate wrought-iron balustrades.

Your eye will first be drawn to the gleaming main altar and half-domed apse area – particularly the golden tabernacle – which features in the Apparitions. Above, and looking down on the tabernacle, is the prominent marble statue of Our Lady – the Virgin of the Radiant Graces – in the attitude she appeared to St Catherine in the main part of the second Apparition, the rays 'of graces' emanating down from her hands.

Chapel of Our Lady of the Miraculous Medal.

She is crowned with an elaborate precious crown, the whole backed by two joined hearts aflame, the twelve stars in a halo above her head, and more rays, splaying outwards over the apse.

As your eye draws back out of the apse you will see the white Carrara marble statue of Our Lady of the Globe, on the right, backed by a swirling blue and white mosaic, bordered by lilies. This is the spot where St Catherine saw this depiction in the first tableau of the second Apparition. Below Our Lady of the Globe is the reliquary of St Catherine Labouré, her body incorrupt, wearing the full habit of the Daughters of Charity. A rosary entwines her hands, steepled together in prayer. In the side altar to the right of this is a statue of St Vincent de Paul, co-founder of the Daughters. At his feet is the golden reliquary containing his heart. The altar front has a fascinating array and arrangement of precious stones. Just to the right of the side chapel is the blue upholstered wooden armchair in which Our Lady sat in the first Apparition, which at the time was placed just to the left of where the main altar is now.

Moving now to the left of the apse, there is a statue of St Joseph with the Child Jesus, similar in style and setting to Our Lady of the Globe. Past St Joseph's statue, is the glass-fronted, gilded bronze reliquary of St Louise de Marillac, co-founder of the Daughters.

Crowning the whole main nave ensemble, and keying in with the statues each side in geometry and colour, is the large semi-circular fresco of the Triumphal Arch, showing aspects of the first Apparition. And if you stand well back and look at this scene as a whole, what may have been a busy, confusing arrangement, now takes on a very pleasing, balanced symmetry of colour, design and description of the events here – all pointing to that glowing tabernacle in the centre.

St Louise de Marillac

"Love the poor and honour them as you would honour Christ Himself."

St Louise de Marillac

Louise de Marillac was born out of wedlock in a prominent French family in 1591. She grew up in affluent circumstances, was well educated, but essentially lacked a conventional, stable 'home life'. Having been refused entry to a religious order, she got married, and had one child, before her husband died prematurely of a chronic illness, having been nursed devotedly by Louise. She had been under the spiritual direction of St Francis de Sales, and after his death felt his promptings to seek out Vincent de Paul for ongoing direction. She was a woman of great intelligence and energy, and whilst still maintaining her household, started developing a spiritual way of life that also embraced caring for the sick and the poor.

She soon found the key to the practicalities of applying this ethos by training humble young women from the countryside who had the ability, energy and right approach for this work, as well as nurturing in them a community spirituality. With her successful work in a major Paris hospital she soon had the reputation for sound organisation that maximised collaboration and teamwork. Under the guidance of St Vincent de Paul, who applied the spiritual dimension, the Daughters of Charity were founded in 1633 as a religious community. Louise's mission to the poor and sick is embodied in St Vincent's words to her: "You will have no veil, save only that of modesty; no cloister, but the streets of the city, the hovels of the poor, the classroom, or the wards of hospitals; your only cell will be a hired room, and your grill, holy obedience."

Louise died in 1660, aged seventy, six months before her great friend and mentor, Vincent de Paul. She was canonised in 1934 by Pope Pius XI. On the third centenary of her death, Pope John XXIII declared her the Patron Saint of Christian Social Workers. Today, over 19,000 Sisters work in 2,275 communities in 91 countries throughout the world.

As you leave the chapel, note the magnificently tiered and balustraded choir and organ gallery. Outside on the rue du Bac, and just round the corner, off the rue de Babylone, are very pleasant public gardens, part bordering the convent wall, providing a pleasant resting or picnic place.

CHAPEL OF SAINT VINCENT DE PAUL

"Charity takes precedence over any rules, everything must be directed towards it, and what it orders should be carried out."

St Vincent de Paul

A short distance from the rue du Bac, on the busy rue de Sèvres, is the church and shrine to St Vincent de Paul (Metro: Vaneau). It has a small, modest front façade with a single entrance, not really giving much indication as to what lies within. This is the final earthly resting place of St Vincent de Paul, missionary to the poor, his remains fittingly laid to rest here in 1830, in the chapel of the Mother House of his Priests of the Congregation of the Mission (also known as the Vincentians or Lazarists).

Saint Vincent de Paul

I have got to admit to taking an immediate liking to St Vincent de Paul just by looking at his picture. He has

St Vincent de Paul.

a kindly-looking, puckish face, with a hint of mischief and humour – but also wisdom and humility about it. But when you read his life story, and see his achievements, you know that behind that, lies a steely and resolute character, but one shot through with love and compassion. Vincent was born into a farming family in southern Gascony, the third of six children, in 1580. His life was one of extraordinary contrasts, and it was not until he was forty five that he found his true calling of serving the poor. He was ordained priest at the early age of twenty; sold into slavery – but gained his freedom by converting his master; and then went on to mix with and work in – for some of the time – the highest echelons of society. His early years are described as 'marked with stoic devotion and earthly goals'.

In working for a particular noble family he was encouraged to minister to the working families on their many estates – really feeling deeply for the first time the physical and spiritual poverty of these people. From here he became a parish priest, where he experienced – after appealing expressively to his congregation to help a needy family – the result of self-empowerment of people willing to help, thus sowing the seeds of how his ministry would eventually operate. Back to Paris, working for the nobility again now gave him the chance, with a large network of influential friends and the finances of a benefactor, to get his mission of tending to the poor finally underway.

He did this specifically in 1625 by forming, from his group of secular priests already living in community, the Congregation of the Mission, spending the next thirty five years expanding this organisation of priests, not only in France, but initially into eight other countries – reaching out to convicts of the galleys, refugees, the victims of epidemics, and the many others afflicted by the unforgiving conditions of war, poverty and sickness. In many ways, he was one of the first to stir the conscience of governments into their responsibility to meeting the needs of the poor and disadvantaged.

From this organisation, others with complementary missions also emerged – the Confraternity of Charity, the Ladies of Charity; he co-founded with St Louise de Marillac, the now worldwide order of the Daughters of Charity of St Vincent de Paul. He was a contemporary of St Francis de Sales, and latterly, spiritual director to St Jane de Chantal and her newly founded Visitandines in Annecy.

He died in his eightieth year in 1660, still firmly 'in harness', working tirelessly tending to his missionary organisations. He was canonised in 1737 by Pope Clement XII, and his feast day is celebrated on 27th September; he is the Patron Saint of all charitable societies.

Chapel

Inside, the chapel is quite gloomy, but is also a peaceful place, elaborately embellished with an ornate, coffered-barrelled ceiling and gleaming, light ochre pillars marching down the sides of the central nave. The downward sweep of the barreled ceiling is pierced with attractive shallow arches of the upper gallery. At the head of the church, high above the imposing, be-statued and niched main altar, you will see the lit reliquary of St Vincent. In the wide arch above the apse is what can only be described as an 'action-packed' frieze of St Vincent ascending to heaven. There are doors each side of the altar, where you can go up to the reliquary, and kneel before it in prayer. The full size, recumbent figure of St Vincent is a wax effigy; his bones are encased in the reliquary. He is fully dressed in his priestly garb, complete with trademark skull cap, with just the hint of a smile on his tired, wise, peaceful face.

Heading each side nave, and either side of the main altar, is a side chapel – to the right, St Joseph, to the left, Our Lady with the Blessed Sacrament, in front of which people are inevitably at prayer. Here there are also shrines and relics of St Francis Regis Clet (1748–1820), and St John Gabriel Perboyre (1802–1840), priests of the Order, both martyred in China. Walking back down you can examine the medallioned windows showing aspects of St Vincent's life with photographic clarity. Next to the statue of Jesus 'passing by the cup', back left of the church, I could not help but smile at the picture of St Vincent rejoicing jubilantly in heaven! There is also a small repository at the back.

Blessed Frederic Ozanam

"I would like to embrace the whole world in a network of charity"

Bl Frederic Ozanam

The direct fruits of St Vincent de Paul have not only endured and grown since his lifetime, but others have sprung up, and also continue to grow, long after his death. One of these such fruits is the renowned and respected international organisation that ministers to the poor, founded by Frederic Ozanam some 175 years later – the Society of St Vincent de Paul (SSVP – or in the case of Australian young people – Vinnies youth!).

Frederic was born in 1813, in Milan, of French-Jewish parents, the fifth of fourteen children, of whom only three survived childhood. The family returned to France in 1815, the parents already engaged in helping the poor; Frederic took this up also. As a student in Paris he became involved with the Daughters of Charity (Blessed Rosalie Rendu), but with the growth of his and his fellow students' charitable activities, he formally founded the fledgling Society in 1835. He was an intelligent and learned man, with a degree in literature and doctorates in law and foreign literature, teaching at the Sorbonne. He was married with one child.

Not always in good health he died in 1853, aged 40; but, by the time of his death he saw his organisation grow to over two thousand chapters world wide. He was beatified by Pope John Paul II in 1997. Today, the Society has some 950,000 members in 132 countries. The genesis of the Society in England and Wales was in 1844; today, there are just over 10,000 members in 1300 Conferences in England and Wales, who, it has been estimated have made 625,000 recorded visits to 110,000 people, amounting to over a million hours of voluntary service. The sister organisation specifically for young people is Youth SSVP, the largest youth organisation in the Church in England and Wales; since 1999 over 10,000 young people have committed themselves to working for the poor and needy.

His relics are in the church of St Joseph des Carmes at the Catholic Institute 70, rue de Vaugirard (Metro: Rennes). Access to the church is through the main entrance of the Catholic Institute. Good knowledge of French would have been a help here, as my enquiry was met with some confusion! However, I did get into the church, and was disappointed in what seemed to be a rather tired and faded building. As I understood it, his relics are in the crypt, to which I could find no access, and there was no-one to ask. It did not seem a fitting place of rest for this man whose legacy is so vibrant today. Maybe I just went on a bad day.

LA MADELEINE

"The Risen Christ [first seen by Mary Magdalene] is indeed at the heart of our faith. Mary Magdalene and the church dedicated to her are here to remind us of this".

La Madeleine Parish Priest

La Madeleine is one of the most unusual and striking churches in Paris, and also has a shrine element, containing a relic of St Mary Magdalene. It was purposely set in the prestigious location of Faubourg Saint Honoré, looking down the rue Royale, south, to

Place de la Concorde (Metro Madeleine). Walking by, and not knowing it to be a church, this huge, monolith of a building, mounted on its immense pedestal and surrounded by fifty two stately Corinthian pillars, could be taken for an important and rather grandiose building of state or high finance.

History

The history and architecture of this church may also sum up the confusion or ambivalence of the French towards the relationship between State and Church. For although it reflects the innate Gallic desire to display a building of great beauty and culture, at varying times it was not known exactly in what direction it was heading! Its planning, development and building started in 1753, when Louis XIV ordered a replacement church.

Between that time and its official inauguration as a church nearly a hundred years later in 1842, it went through many forms and purposes, designs, pull-downs and rebuilds, according to the mood of the time: starting as a church, then a meeting place for the Assembly during the Revolution, then a Temple of the Revolution, then Napoleon wanted a Temple to the glory of the Grande Armée; finally Louis XVIII restored the building for religious purposes (though exactly what purpose was still not clear) in 1815. Now,

La Madeleine.

its principal function is humble parish church, of one of the 110 parishes in Paris, but is also a centre for many other religious and cultural events on a national scale.

Exterior

The Neo-Classical exterior speaks quite simply but majestically for itself – the great, sentinel, uniform march of the pillars round the building; but notice also the many larger-than-life-size statues of the saints that inhabit the niches of the two lateral porticos – fourteen down each side. Before ascending the wide sweep of the stairs, look up at the pediment depicting Christ banishing on His left, the Vices, and on His right encouraging the Virtues. Mary Magdalene kneels in repentance at His left side. Then look up to the impressive bronze doors – larger than those of St Peter's, Rome, and displaying finely worked panels of eight of the commandments – the first two are on the impost above, with Moses central, holding aloft the tablet.

Inside

Inside, there is again, a fundamental simplicity of expression, but richly embellished – a large single nave, topped by three domes spanning wide, arched bays. The temple theme is continued with the sizeable Corinthian pillars down the sides of the nave and smaller ones round the apse. Looking down the church you will see ahead of you the splendid composition and combination – in the sanctuary and apse – of statue, mosaic and fresco.

The statue over the main altar is the Ecstasy of St Mary Magdalene, with Mary, arms wide in submission, her soft face radiating tranquility, being gently uplifted by three surrounding angels. Tradition has it that Mary Magdalene ended her days in Provence, at St Baume, and was often visited by angels. The mosaic round the barrel of the apse shows Christ in His glory, flanked left and right by the evangelisers of France, many of whom by tradition came to France soon after the Resurrection. The whole is crowned by the tumultuous apse fresco portraying the history and glory of Christianity: Jesus central, hand raised in blessing, to, on His right, many characters of the Western Church throughout the ages, and on His left, the Eastern Church.

Reliquaries

Each side of the sanctuary are the ornate silver gilt and enamel reliquaries studded with precious stones of, on the left, St Vincent de Paul, and on the right, Mary Magdalene. There are three side altars each side in each bay of the nave, above which are detailed paintings of aspects of Mary Magdalene's life. There are two side chapels at the rear of the church. I was very taken with the one on the left as you go out – in which there is a powerful, moving, descriptive statue of the Wedding of Our Lady – a subject which one never really gives much thought to. Mary, demure, eyes downcast; Joseph looking adoringly at her, gently holding her hand; the impressive high priest – central – left hand and forefinger lifted heavenwards, right hand spread wide over the couple, giving the blessing.

On leaving this magnificent building it is hard to believe that it is a parish church. Yet a walk round the outside, looking at the various entrances beneath the church, reveals all sorts of outreach activities being conducted by the parish.

ST AUGUSTINE'S CHURCH

"Let us be persons of desire and of prayer. Let us never believe anything to be impossible: God can do all."

Charles de Foucauld

Conveniently, St Augustine's is a short stroll from La Madeleine, down Boulevard Malesherbes (Metro St-Augustin). I am suggesting St Augustine's as an appropriate venue, because it is closely associated with Blessed Charles de Foucauld, and comes as near as there is to a shrine commemorating him in France, although there is evidence of him at the Sacré-Coeur, and no doubt other churches in France. St Augustine's also has some unique architectural features.

Blessed Charles de Foucauld

A full account of Charles de Foucauld's fascinating life is given in the CTS booklet *'Charles de Foucauld'*. He was born in Strasbourg in 1858 of a noble family, but orphaned as a young child. He went to St Cyr Military Academy in 1876, and having finished training joined a crack cavalry regiment, enjoying a life of youthful excess as the glamorous Viscount de Foucauld. Tiring of army life, but fascinated with North Africa where he had served, he left the army in 1882, and made a name for himself as a respected and courageous explorer, being awarded a Gold Medal by the Paris Geographic Society for his explorations of Morocco.

Returning to France in 1886, he stayed with his aunt's family close to St Augustine's church. He was already questioning his loss and lack of faith, asking, "My God, if you exist, let me come to know you". This was answered through the Parish Priest of St Augustine, Fr Huvelin, who took him under his wing, giving spiritual direction, infusing the belief that Charles was seeking. His subsequent discernment of vocation was long and varied: pilgrimage to the Holy Land, Trappist monk for seven years, gardener to the Poor Clare convent in Nazareth, finally ordained priest in 1901.

He returned to his beloved North Africa where wanted to be among those who were, "the furthest removed, the most abandoned." He lived first in Beni Abbès and later at Tamanrasset among the Tuaregs of the Hoggar. In a raid by Tuaregs on his fort on the 1st of December 1916, he was shot dead in the ensuing melee.

Although his desire to form religious communities during his lifetime did not materialise, his life and death inspired the formation of congregations and groups which derived their inspiration, purpose, and Rules from Charles de Foucauld. Amongst them are the Little Brothers of Jesus, and Little Sisters of Jesus, who live in small fraternal groups all over the world, preaching simply through the way they live their lives.

Church with a difference

This church does not appear as big as it is standing close up – but its large, gleaming, slate-covered dome, topped by its distinctive russet coloured lantern, is plainly visible amongst the clutter of buildings when viewed from the far off dome of the Sacré-Coeur. The church, described as 'vaguely Byzantine' in style, was built between 1860 and 1869, being solemnly consecrated in 1879. It was built on a trapezium-shaped plot of land, and the footprint of the church reflects this – narrower from the front façade (19 metres), gradually

St Augustine's Church.

widening to a not insubstantial 39 metres at the sanctuary. This is not immediately evident, as, inside, the nave is straight and uniform; it is the side chapels that bear the increasing width.

Two other novel features of this church are, firstly, the use of metal framework, clearly visible throughout by the supporting columns, but particularly at the top of the arches, in the form of attractive, swirling metalwork patterns. This metal structure obviated the need for extra supporting stone pillars creating side naves, which limits visibility. It was the first sizeable religious building in Paris to employ this method of construction. Secondly, but not at all obvious, is that the dome is actually a dome within a dome – the inner cupola being separated by quite a considerable space from the separate, outer dome.

Side chapels and Sanctuary

A series of side chapels, one of which is the church 'accueil', flank the nave. The one of interest in this context, dedicated to Blessed Charles de Foucauld, commemorates his conversion in this church, and provides a charming display of pictures, aspects and artifacts of his life.

As you approach the sanctuary area you will not help but notice the elaborate, striking *baldacchino* above the original altar, executed in this instance in the style of a hanging ciborium. A large, modern, red copper and gilded cross, backed by a lengthy drape, hangs here. Looking on up at the cupola, the metal framework, with its triple columns supporting the inner cupola, is evident, reaching up past the clear windows to the vault paintings of Christ in His glory, Our Lady, and characters from the Old and New Testaments. Note also the handsome, moulded figures of angels adorning the supporting metal columns.

Three more side chapels open from the sanctuary – from the left, St Joseph; the axial, or chevet chapel – as one would expect, is the Lady Chapel, in which resides the Blessed Sacrament. It is a lovely chapel, with a richly mosaiced altar, bright stained glass windows, elaborate wrought-iron arches, and is a lovely place for a few moments of quiet prayer. The last chapel, on the right, is dedicated to the Sacred Heart of Jesus. On your way back out of the church you will see at the rear, the conventional arrangement of a large rose window with the serried ranks of organ pipes, below.

As with La Madeleine this is a parish church serving its parishioners, evidenced by the rooms in the crypt underneath – used for services on cold winter days, for social gatherings and for teaching catechism. A memorable church with a difference – but serving the same purpose.

❧ BURGUNDY ❧

NEVERS

"My own concerns no longer concern me: from now on I must entirely belong to God, and God alone. Never to myself."

St Bernadette

Nevers is a medium sized town, almost in the centre of France, directly off the N7, and some 45 miles east of Bourges. It sits on high ground overlooking the Loire, with the cathedral, and its tall, blunt tower, dominating the old part of the town. It is well known for its distinctive high-fired pottery and handsome 15th century Gothic Ducal Palace, overlooking the river.

In Catholic pilgrimage terms it is an important and popular destination, housing the relics of St Bernadette in the convent to where she came from Lourdes, and in which she spent the last thirteen years of her life. A 'snapshot' account is given of her in the 'Lourdes' section of this booklet; for more detail there are several CTS booklets dealing with aspects of her life and spirituality, and Lourdes.

L'Espace Bernadette Soubirous

L'Espace Bernadette is the former convent, St Gildard's, of the Sisters of Charity of Nevers, the

Order that Bernadette joined. Today it fulfills the function of receiving the hundreds of thousands of pilgrims every year who come to venerate the relics of St Bernadette. It is set in extensive grounds just to the north of the old part of the town. It is still run by the Sisters, who are augmented from other houses from many parts of the world to cope with the increased numbers of pilgrims during the high season. If you head straight to the information booth (*accueil*) on arrival, you will receive a warm welcome from the Sister on duty (not necessarily in English!), and also gather what information you need for your visit.

Chapel and Reliquary

The focus, initially, of all the pilgrims, is the small, intimate convent chapel where Bernadette's incorrupt body is on view in the side chapel reliquary (*chasse*). You will see it almost on entry, in the right-hand side chapel. Her recumbent body, in the ornate gilt-enamel, glass fronted reliquary, lit from inside, is fully clothed in the habit of the Order. Her head is gently tilted to the left, her hands, holding a rosary, folded on her breast. Although her body is incorrupt, her hands and face have been covered with a light wax mask to maintain colour. Her serene face radiates a picture of absolute peace and tranquility. The chapel is subtly lit, with natural light coming in from the

St Bernadette.

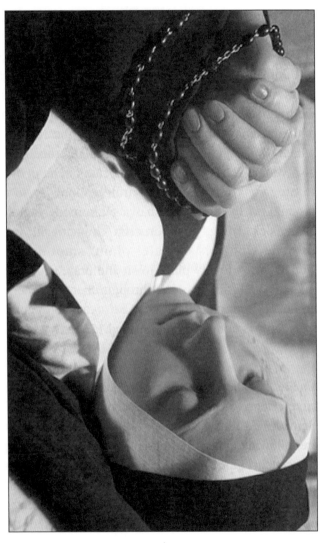

narrow modern stained glass windows above; a statue of Our Lady and the Child Jesus look on.

The convent chapel itself is simple – understated. It has a long, narrow, single nave, with modern stained glass windows, high up, letting in light. There is a well-defined transept, and to the left of the sanctuary is the matching apsidal chapel to the reliquary, and in which resides the Blessed Sacrament. The sanctuary is also simple – five-sided, with delicate pillars dividing to elegant arches for the windows and up to the groining of the ceiling. It has a plain modern granite altar, backed by a large Crucifix, dramatically back-lit. The whole is of pale, plain, smooth-faced stonework. A lovely place to sit and pray, and despite the many pilgrims passing through, there is generally an air of quiet and reverence. Be aware that entry to the chapel is not permitted during Masses.

Garden Walk

One of the other main features is being able to walk the quite extensive convent grounds, much as they were in Bernadette's time; it is quite a thrill knowing that you are following in her footsteps. You can pick up a loaned self-conduct guide folder from the reception booth (for a small donation), which will take you round. I found it well structured, informative and thought-provoking, as you contemplate at various places, Bernadette's commitment, spirituality and other aspects of her life. Of particular note is the ivy-clad grotto in the far corner of the garden, in which is Our Lady of the Waters, a statue that Bernadette said was very similar to Our Lady of Lourdes, and where she often prayed. Almost at the end of the garden tour is the small chapel of St Joseph where Bernadette was initially buried.

Other Features

Within the complex there is also a small **museum** – modern, and tastefully presenting various aspects of Bernadette's life. One rather amusing item was her snuff box, which apparently, in those times, people with chest complaints were encouraged to use! Judging by the size of her clothes on display, she was also very petite. In the area facing the chapel is a full-size and well constructed replica of the **grotto at Lourdes** – the familiar statue of Our Lady of Lourdes in the niche up high, a plain stone altar and a blaze of votive candles in the main grotto. A well stocked **shop** and bookshop is on hand, as are toilets. Simple pilgrim accommodation is available in the old convent for those pilgrims wishing to extend their stay. A DVD of Bernadette's life – in English – can also be viewed on request at the *accueil*, depending on other viewing requirements. A well-organised, warmly welcoming place, in which you can quietly drift around at your leisure.

Other places in Nevers

In the pilgrim context there are other places of interest in Nevers, which if you have time, are worth dropping in on. The **Cathedral of Saint Cyr-Sainte Juliette** is an absolute must. One does get a bit blasé when visiting a lot of these splendid buildings, and, expecting a 'standard cathedral' quick tour and tick it off, I was flabbergasted once inside! Apart from anything – it is vast! You could regard this as work in progress, as this church has been continuously evolving since the 6th century, and various architectural aspects obviously reflect this. The two principal ones are the double apse, one at each end: at the western end, Romanesque 11th century with its 12th century fresco, and eastern end, Gothic. The other obvious feature – love them or loathe them – is the most spectacular display of modern stained glass windows, to which various craftspeople were invited to contribute their efforts to replace the bomb damage of the Second World War. Unity of theme there is not – blaze of light and colour there is!

Two churches are within reasonable walking distance within the town: the 17th century **Saint Pierre** in the shape of a Greek cross (with even 'arms') with its trompe-l'oeil frescoes; and then the venerable 11th century **Saint Etienne**, built in the Cluniac style, with its striking architectural arrangement of the chapels at the chevet end. Those of you who have been to Paray-le-Monial will see a remarkable similarity.

Lastly, a mile or so north of the old town, just off the D907, the most extraordinarily shaped, modern church that I suspect you will ever see. This is the church of **Sainte Bernadette du Banlay**. Its grim, foreboding exterior, with not a window in sight, and its shuttered concrete clam-like shell, makes it look just like a nuclear bomb shelter. Frustratingly, opening hours were not evident, so I did not have the benefit of looking inside at the architect's concept of *'fonction oblique'* – which declares that buildings should be all about ramps, slopes and angles, wall-free where possible, and that space should predominate over surface. How that translates into the interior of this church, I shall probably never know – but it is intriguing!

PARAY-LE-MONIAL

"In the seventeenth century the Lord chose your town to bring forth a new source of merciful and infinitely generous love on which generations of pilgrims would draw."

Pope John Paul II

The name may not mean much to you – nor did it to me, until I started my pilgrim journeys through France. In this context it is a significant place – being where the 'modern' devotion to the Sacred Heart of Jesus started, inspired by the direct wishes of Our Lord conveyed to St Margaret Mary Alacoque, a young nun in the town's convent of the Visitandine Order, in 1673.

The Town

Paray is some 65 miles north west of Lyon, just off the N79/E62. It is a delightful place, well off the mass tourist trail, and thus untouched by today's corporate branding, still retaining its original identity. There is plenty for the pilgrim here to do and see, as well as enjoy a quiet little corner of France in this engaging town, with its extensive public gardens – large and small – and its partly pedestrianised old town, all neat as a pin and full of character.

Probably its original claim to fame in more distant history is the arrival of the Benedictines in 973 and onwards, developing and building their community – of which the current visible reminder is the lovely 11th century Romanesque basilica dedicated to the Sacred Heart.

Saint Margaret Mary Alacoque

*"Lord Jesus, let my heart never rest until it finds
You, who are its centre, its love, and its
happiness."*

Prayer of St Margaret Mary Alacoque

Margaret Mary was born in 1647, in the Burgundy
village of L'Hautecour, the fifth child of seven. In
many ways her circumstances were similar to St
Thérèse of Lisieux – losing a parent at an early age
and suffering a debilitating disease, of which
through the intercession of Our Lady, she was cured.
Latterly, like Thérèse, she achieved worldwide
recognition, having been an anonymous, cloistered
nun during her lifetime.

She resisted family pressure for marriage, having
felt called to the religious life, and entered the
Visitandine Order convent in 1671, aged twenty-four.
In the eighteen months starting on 27th December
1673, Margaret Mary started experiencing the
encounters with Christ that would clarify and specify
her mission to the world – that of spreading the
devotion to His Sacred Heart; He said to her, "Its
needs must be spread abroad by means of yourself,
and so manifest itself to all to enrich them with the
treasure this Heart contains". Our Lord also gave her

very precise instructions as to how this was to be achieved and what form this was to take – the basis of today's specific devotions (see CTS booklet *'Devotion to the Sacred Heart'* for details).

Somewhat daunted by the seeming impossibility of this task – particularly in view of the scepticism and opposition of her Superior and some of her fellow Sisters – she was nonetheless assured by Our Lord that a special advocate would be sent to her. He came in the form of Father Claude de la Colombière, a Jesuit priest, who was providentially appointed chaplain and confessor to the convent. On meeting him she heard the inner voice, "He it is I send you". Father Claude had no doubts as to the credibility of her encounters, and with him as confidant and supporter, her strength grew again in the belief of her mission. And through Fr Claude, subsequently supported wholeheartedly by his Order – the Society of Jesus – the devotion of the Sacred Heart has been taken to every corner of the earth.

Later on, a change of Superior, and of attitude, allowed the devotion also to spread from the convent to other Visitandine houses and Orders, establishing it from within and from its source. She died of an illness, aged 43, in 1690, secure in the knowledge that the instructions that Our Lord gave her were faithfully being implemented on a wide scale. In 1920 she was canonised by Pope Benedict XV, and her feast day is celebrated by the Universal Church on the 16th of October. As instructed by Our Lord, the feast of the Sacred Heart is celebrated on the Friday after the octave of Corpus Christi, also nineteen days after Pentecost. St Margaret Mary's reliquary is in the convent chapel of the Visitation in Paray.

Saint Claude de la Colombière

"In You, O Lord, I have hoped; never let me be confounded."

Prayer of St Claude de la Columbière

Claude de la Colombière was born in 1641. He was an intelligent, gifted and well-connected young man, who chose the priesthood to use his gifts, being ordained into the Jesuits, where a bright future, particularly in the academic world, lay ahead of him. Subsequently, in a somewhat puzzling move, he was sent to the seeming backwater of Paray. However, with his encounters with Sister Margaret Mary, he soon realised that he was the 'faithful servant and perfect friend' that Our Lord had promised her.

His tenure at the convent was only eighteen months, but long enough to establish the credibility and veracity of Margaret Mary's visions, and to give the initial impetus to the spread of the message. In another puzzling move, no doubt through his family's noble connections, he was sent to London as tutor and preacher to Mary of Modena, Duchess of York, in 1676. In what was a political and spiritual minefield, ministering to this royal Catholic family in Protestant England, Fr Claude is reported as preaching sensitively, but without compromise. He also preached on the Sacred Heart, and subsequently Mary, as exiled Queen of England in France, petitioned the Holy See to establish the Feast of the Sacred Heart.

His stay in England was just as brief. Being implicated in a 'Popish plot' to assassinate Charles II he was imprisoned, only being released through the direct intervention of Louis XIV. Being not in good health, and his time in prison having taken further toll, he died in Paray in 1682, aged 41. He was canonised by Pope John Paul II in 1992. His reliquary is in the attractive Jesuit chapel built in his memory, in Paray.

Pilgrim places in Paray

Chapel of the Visitation: The heart of your visit to Paray will lie here in this simple convent chapel, where Margaret Mary had her visions of Jesus. It remains a simple monastery chapel for the Sisters. A large fresco on the apse wall depicts the vision of Jesus revealing His Sacred Heart to Margaret Mary. You will also notice the beautiful free-standing tabernacle, in the shape of a large, gracefully curved and open silver heart, topped by a silver cross. In the small, brightly-lit side chapel on the right near the altar rails, is the reliquary of St Margaret Mary, in which lies the fully habited wax image of her, at rest and at peace. Her unseen relics are placed in the reliquary. Inside the sanctuary and to the right you will see the large metal grille through which the enclosed nuns of the Order can participate in Mass and other public liturgies. To the left, just off the sanctuary, is a side altar dedicated to Our Lady. It is lovely to go to Mass here, encouraging to see the number of young people attending, uplifting to listen to the singing, peaceful to join the sisters for their daily liturgy, or just to sit, contemplating or praying during the quiet moments. There is a small shop attached to the chapel.

Basilica of the Sacred Heart: This handsome, twin-towered 11th century church sits prominently on the town's riverside. It is the third church on this site, all built by the Benedictines. The current church, built in Romanesque style, was started in 1092, being completed in the 13th century. The bluff, fairly plain architecture at front and sides, turns to a marvellous tumbling architectural cascade of stone and tile, at the back, with the chevet arrangement of side chapels, typical of the Cluny style. Inside, it is light and lofty, with its bright, butter-coloured pillars and arches and the plain, dazzling white walls and vaulted ceiling; the light inside, as the sun passes over the church, providing a soft luminosity. The church has a lovely harmony, quite delicate in places. The Lady Chapel in the south transept, the only part of the church with a Gothic style, houses the Blessed Sacrament, and also displays a powerful Pietà: a lovely place to pray. Note also the chapel of St Michael the Archangel, above the porch at the rear part of the second church, and slightly out of alignment from the main church. You may gain access to the small, neat, cloister garden through the arch in the building façade to the right of the basilica.

Espace St Jean: Just at the back of the basilica is the helpful Pilgrim Information Office, where you can request to see a DVD, in English, on St Margaret Mary. Opposite is a well stocked pilgrim shop, but with few English publications. Down the side of the basilica is an obliging Tourist Information Office.

Adoration Chapel: Above the Espace St Jean is the tranquil simple, barn-like Chapel of St John, in which is held continuous adoration, night and day.

The Green Cathedral.

Green Cathedral: Also behind the basilica, denoted by the sign *'Parc des Chapelains'*, is a large, park-like area, with many mature trees planted in the pattern of a church, with a long, stately nave-like avenue leading up to the 'transept' area, in which stands the only stone feature, a dome, providing the sanctuary with apse and altar. Over to the left, there is a charming diorama presentation about the life and times of St Margaret Mary Alacoque. Around the Green Cathedral, you can follow the Stations of the Cross; note also the dramatic grotto of Jesus in Gethsemane. In front of the presbytery, a graceful statue of Our Lady faces down the nave towards the altar. A beautiful church, made by man and nature, in which to sit – if the weather is on your side – and listen to the peace.

Chapel of St Claude de la Colombière: In a quiet corner of the town is the chapel built in 1929 by the Jesuits to commemorate St Claude on his beatification. The rather conventional façade belies what lies within! What, on first impression, seems an architectural hotch-potch, gradually emerges, with patient examination, as an intriguing and beguiling church that really catches the imagination! The church is renowned for its truly splendid, vibrant mosaics – apse and side chapels, front and rear. The focus, though, is the reliquary in the left hand transept, atop which is the graceful, recumbent figure of St Claude in soft, rich, gleaming brass, hands joined in prayer. Beneath that, in the brass and pink-marbled reliquary, are his bones and skull, plainly visible. I found this a very simple, dignified and moving setting in which to quietly and reflectively pray, giving thanks for St Claude's significant ministry of the Sacred Heart.

PONTIGNY

Just north east of Auxerre, on the N77, and about nine miles north of the village of Chablis, is the solid, long, red-tiled **Cistercian abbey church** of Pontigny, standing out proud from the surrounding countryside. Indeed, the monks had an association with Chablis, as amongst their labours they are said to have helped establish the original vineyards around Chablis. In the context of the British pilgrim it is of interest, because here lie the mortal remains of **St Edmund Rich of Abingdon** (1175 – 1240), former Archbishop of Canterbury.

Although Edmund was a gentle, pious and austere man, he fiercely defended the rights of Church and State against the exactions and usurpations of Henry III, finding himself embattled on all sides, including from Rome. Utterly frustrated, he retired to Pontigny

The Abbey of Pontigny.

to live the life of a simple religious, dying soon after. He was canonised in 1247 after reported miracles occurred at his graveside.

Inside, the abbey is beautiful, austere and bare – devoid of any substantial colour – just stonework from flagged floor to vaulted ceiling, probably as one would expect of a Cistercian abbey. His tomb is at the end of the apse in the abbey.

VEZELAY

"Has not the builder, fascinated by the beauty of the universe which he recognises as the work of God, erected this vestibule to Heaven in imitation of God who created with order, measure and beauty?"

Father Hugues Delautre on Vezelay abbey

Some 130 kms west of Dijon, 15 kms off the A6/E15 in the Department of Yonne in Burgundy, stands the magnificent **Benedictine 12th century abbey church of St Mary Magdalene** – 'La Madeleine'. It sits fortress-like, in a dominating hill-top position. The abbey was an important gathering point for pilgrims heading to Santiago de Compostela during the Middle Ages, and is now a UNESCO World Heritage Site. It is particularly noted for its intricate Romanesque sculpted imagery, particularly the three tympanums in the narthex, and the 99 finely carved capitals throughout the church.

History of La Madeleine

The original monastery was established here about 860, and was destroyed in the early 10th century by marauding Normans. It was soon refounded, along with claims from the monks that they had acquired the relics of Mary Magdalene, which immediately started attracting pilgrims, particularly those on their way to Santiago. Construction started on the present abbey in 1120, with the overly-large narthex being added from 1140 to accommodate ever increasing pilgrim numbers.

It was also a meeting point for the great and the good – the abbey community was then a prominent and influential establishment, with its 800 or so monks. Saint Bernard of Clairvaux preached here at Easter 1146 supporting the Second Crusade, in front of King Louis VII. Richard I of England and Philip II of France spent three months together in 1190 before leaving for the Third Crusade. Thomas Becket whilst in exile chose Vézelay for his Whitsunday sermon in 1166, announcing the excommunication of the main supporters of the

English King, Henry II, also threatening the King with excommunication.

The 13th century saw the serious decline of Vézelay, after the authenticity of Mary Magdalene's relics was challenged in favour of those discovered at St-Maximin-La-Ste-Baume in Provence in 1279 (see also La-Ste-Baume in the chapter on Provence). The decline continued until only 15 monks were left in the community by 1537. During the Wars of Religion Vézelay became a Huguenot stronghold, with the abbey being used as a barracks, granary and hay store. It was returned to the Church in 1569.

Although damage to the abbey itself during the French Revolution was not overly severe, lack of maintenance and neglect over the years rendered it in danger of collapse. A remarkable rescue of the structure was effected by a young architect, Viollet-le-Duc, between 1840 and 1859, who successfully took on a task that no established architect was willing to accept – stability was re-imposed by the enterprising addition of flying buttresses to support the nave. The pilgrimage movement re-gathered momentum when the Archbishop of Sens donated relics of Mary Magdalene in 1870 and 1876.

Abbey

The interior of this church, with its capacious narthex, Romanesque nave and Gothic sanctuary and apse is strikingly beautiful with its subtle simplicity only serving to emphasise its glorious loft and length – the whole is only a few yards shorter than Notre Dame cathedral in Paris. It is lighter inside than most Romanesque churches, owing to the clear, high, clerestory windows and the generous window space of the sanctuary. The throw of sunlight from the clerestory windows plays a particularly important part on the two solstices: on the summer solstice the nine distinct pools of light shine directly down into the centre of the nave aligning precisely with the centre of the sanctuary; on the winter solstice the sunshine perfectly illuminates the capitals on the north wall of the clerestory. The abbey was aligned specifically to achieve this: the summer solstice being the feast of the birth of John the Baptist, the winter solstice the Nativity.

The simple, smooth, gleaming flagstones complement perfectly the honey coloured, translucent limestone stonework of the interior, with its graceful columns, headed by carved capitals, which in turn support the striking 'striped' arches. The ambulatory round the sanctuary and the five side chapels give an

Abbey church of St Mary Magdalene.

air of space and grace – portraying a place of elegant simplicity. The Carolingian crypt holds the relics of Mary Magdalene presented by the Archbishop of Sens. On the terrace behind the church there are magnificent views of the countryside below. The abbey is served by the Monastic Fraternities of Jerusalem founded in 1975 to promote the 'spirit of the monastic desert in the cities', in keeping with Charles de Foucauld's vision.

CLUNY

Cluny is a small town in the Saône-et-Loire department, 90 kms north of Lyon, and 50 kms directly east from Paray-le-Monial. It was here that a **Benedictine abbey** was founded in 910, and from which significant reforming influence was exerted on western monasticism, radiating across western Europe between the 10th and 14th centuries.

The Development of Cluny

Three successive abbeys were built on the present site – known as Cluny I, II and III. William I of Aquitaine endowed the lands on which Cluny I was built, starting in 910. This endowment was unusual at the time, as he freed the abbot from any of the usual feudal obligations towards him and his successors, other than that of prayer. A succession of highly astute and competent abbots, of whom four subsequently became Popes and four were canonised, guided the development of Cluny in three directions: the primacy of the liturgy as the major activity of their vocation, the establishment of an ever growing number of dependent monasteries (known as priories) throughout western Europe, all held directly under the authority of the Abbot of Cluny, and the prohibition of any land or property that they held being subject to secular or feudal authority.

Cluny I was destroyed in 953 by marauding Hungarians, and the construction of Cluny II started soon after. As a manifestation of Cluny's influence and growth, the construction of Cluny III was initiated by its sixth abbot, St Hugh, in 1089, and was consecrated by Pope Innocent II in 1130. It was the largest church in Christendom before the new St Peter's in Rome was built five centuries later, and boasted five naves, a narthex and several towers; with its associated buildings, it covered an area of twenty-five acres. Its Romanesque architectural style, particularly its distinctive chevet cluster of protruding side chapels surrounding the sanctuary, was copied in many abbeys throughout France – the Basilica of the Sacred Heart at nearby Paray-le-Monial being a prime example.

The monastery was also an important stopping-off point for pilgrims en route to Santiago via le Puy-en-Velay, and from it, the Benedictine rule of hospitality spread to its own priories, and other pilgrim hospices along the Way of St James, with the dictum of 'never knowing whether the next wayfarer was a humble pilgrim or Christ himself'.

Decline of Cluny

At the height of its influence in the 12th century Cluny held sway over some 314 monasteries with their 10,000 monks in France, England, Scotland, Italy and Poland. In England there were thirty-five Cluniac houses at the time of dissolution, the first being established at Lewes by William de Warenne between 1078 and 1082, dedicated to St Pancras. There were three priories established in Scotland.

The early 12th century started seeing the decline of Cluny's wide ranging influence. Poor governance at the time contributed, as did the emergence of other mendicant orders and the Cistercians, ushering in a new wave of ecclesiastical reform. The emergence of England and France as sovereign states also mitigated against the Cluniac model, with resistance to an abbot in Burgundy ruling widely dispersed houses. The abbey's fortunes also suffered during the civil and religious wars of the 16th century.

Abbey of Cluny.

The Cluny movement was strongly identified with the 'Ancient Regime' during the French Revolution, and the order was suppressed. The abbey suffered grievously during the Revolution. Most of its extensive and precious library was burned, land was sold off, and the abbey building was largely demolished, serving as a quarry for local construction.

Today

Although one can trace the outlines of the abbey, giving an idea of size and scale, all that is left standing is the towers of the **Porte d'Honneur**, the entrance to the abbey from the village, and the **Clocher de l'Eau-Bénite**, the smaller tower over the remains of the south transept. On one side of what was the transept are some graceful **18th century cloisters**. There is also a 13th century Gothic building which served on the lower level as a wine store, and on the upper level as a granary. The granary has a beautiful 13th century oak and chestnut barrel-vaulted roof which serves as a small **museum**, housing artifacts from Cluny III, amongst which are eight Romanesque capitals and their columns.

Gone is that great building, never to be replaced. Gone is its immediate influence – but a powerful legacy lives on. And in having a peaceful and meditative wander around the environs, and recalling the significant impact and size of Cluny, one may just begin to feel and hear the distant chanting and the prayers of those many hundreds of monks.

AUVERGNE AND
～ RHÔNE ALPS ～

ARS-SUR-FORMANS

*"The Curé of Ars stands for all nations as an
incomparable model both of the fulfillment of the
ministry and of the holiness of the minister."*

Pope John Paul II

The Village of Ars

Like the many hundreds of other small nondescript
villages buried away in rural France, time and history
would have passed Ars by, had it not been for its
extraordinary parish priest, John-Mary Vianney, who
ministered to this village for forty years between
1818 and 1859, and now known world-wide as 'the
Curé of Ars'.

The village, some twenty miles north of Lyon, and
just east of Villefranche-sur-Saône off the A6/E15, is
the archetypal, sleepy 'one street village', buried in
rural quiet. It has very few tourist facilities or
amenities, being centred entirely round its role as a
world-wide pilgrim venue. It is conveniently a very
compact site, all its aspects being within very easy
walking reach of each other, and all giving a
comprehensive feel for the extraordinary ministry of
the Curé and the impact he had on the village, France

and the world. There is plenty for the serious pilgrim, or the simply curious, to do and see.

St John-Mary Vianney

Born in 1786, John Vianney's life and times are fully described in the CTS booklet *'John Vianney'*. Suffice to say it reads like a roller coaster of adversity, faith, self-sacrificing single-mindedness and relentless endeavour – all achieved with gentle love. In coming to Ars in 1818 – having struggled to attain ordination to the priesthood – he was faced with a congregation made apathetic to the Faith by the strictures of the Revolution. But by dint of personal example and pastoral devotion to his parishioners and the poor, as well as good old fashioned self-denial, fiery, non-compromising sermonising and exhortation, he gradually gained a reputation for integrity, sincerity and sanctity – a reputation that eventually spread well beyond the village, with thousands coming from all over France, and beyond, to hear his preaching and to confess to him.

He is described as being a 'martyr' to his confessional, spending up to eighteen hours a day in it, and he was well known for his gift of 'reading souls' as people came to him. He died on 4th August 1859, aged 73, was canonised by Pope Pius X in 1925, and in 1929 he was declared Patron Saint of all

Ars - the Basilica.

Parish Priests by Pius XI. His Feast is celebrated by the Universal Church on 4th August.

Pilgrim Places in Ars

Basilica: The village is dominated – but not overwhelmed – by the small, neat basilica with its green copper domes. It presents a lovely, seamless joining together of the old, simple, original 12th century parish church – much as the Curé knew it – with the modern, elaborate, pale-stoned and domed basilica, consecrated in 1885. Two additional side chapels, placed between the two, were added in 1905, on the occasion of the beatification of John-Mary. The right hand side chapel contains the reliquary, in which the incorrupt body of St John Vianney is placed in view, and is the focus of visiting pilgrims.

The Curé's presbytery: Left virtually as it was in his time, with interesting artefacts of his, including his bed which the devil set on fire!

Reception (*Accueil*): Efficiently and cheerfully run by the Benedictine Sisters of the Sacred Heart of Montmartre; and next door,

Votive candle chapel: in which is the famous, iconic statue by Cabuchet of the kneeling Curé;

Chapel of the Heart: Contains the incorrupt heart of John-Mary in a beautiful reliquary;

Church of Our Lady of Mercy: largely out of sight, the sizeable underground, modern and functional 'overflow' church.

Adoration chapel of the Providence: which John-Mary established as a place of Eucharistic Adoration, and helped build.

Wax works diorama: depicting the life and times of John-Mary.

If you are on pilgrimage and staying overnight, the very reasonable pilgrim residence and former orphanage founded by the Curé, **'la Providence'**, is close by. Just outside the village is the seminary and **Foyer Sacerdotal John Paul II** for priests on retreat; the modern chapel is open to the public, and is well worth a visit. Less than a mile out of town is the **Monument of the Encounter** where having received directions to Ars from a young shepherd boy, the Curé advised him, "You have shown me the way to Ars, I will show you the way to heaven".

"Here is a rule for everyday life: do not do anything which you cannot offer to God."

St John-Mary Vianney

ANNECY

"A man of great goodness and kindness, who knew how to express God's mercy and patience to those who came to speak with him, he taught an exacting but serene spirituality based on love..."

Pope John Paul II on St Francis de Sales

Annecy is a bustling holiday resort town in the Haute-Savoie, set well on the tourist trail because of its picturesque setting on the northern shores of Lake Annecy. It has an appealing mediaeval quarter, with largely pedestrianised narrow ancient streets, interspersed with Venetian type canals lapping up against the buildings. Rather surprisingly it is twinned with Cheltenham!

In amongst it all there is, however, a treasure-trove of pilgrim spots, because this is the home and final resting place of two notable French saints of the early 17th century – St Francis de Sales, known as 'the Doctor of Love', and St Jane Frances de Chantal – co-founders of the Institute of the Visitation of the Blessed Virgin, a religious order of nuns more commonly known as the Visitandines. Their lives are reflected today through a contrasting and fascinating variety of churches in this town.

St Francis de Sales

A full account of St Francis de Sales's life is given in the CTS booklet *'Francis de Sales'*. He was an extraordinarily talented but humble man – born the eldest son of a noble Savoyard family in 1567, he turned his back on family expectations of marriage and continuing noble life, to become a priest, being ordained in 1583. It was also evident early on that he was extremely erudite, with the gift of persuasive oratory and clear, concise writing. Combining his formidable intellect with a very practical and hands-on and pastoral approach – both as priest, and latterly as Bishop of Geneva, based in Annecy (1602) – he was an outstanding leader of the Counter-Reformation. He made great inroads into converting people from Calvinism, as well as enlightening the faithful with his marvellous treatises, both spoken and written, of which the CTS booklets *'Love of God'* and *'Letters to a Wife and Mother'* give but a flavour. St Francis and St Jane de Chantal were both contemporaries of St Vincent de Paul.

He died, aged 55, on 28 December 1622 in Lyon, and was canonised in 1665 by Pope Alexander VII. In recognition of his many learned writings he was made a Doctor of the Church by Pius IX in 1877. His feast is celebrated by the Universal Church on 24th January. He is patron saint of writers and the Catholic press. The Order of the Salesians of Don Bosco, founded by St John Bosco in 1859 is named after him, as are the Oblates of St Francis de Sales founded in 1871, and the Missionaries of St Francis de Sales (MSFS) founded in 1830.

St Jane Frances de Chantal

"Once we have humbled ourselves for our faults that God allows us to become aware of in ourselves, we must forget them and go forward."

St Jane de Chantal

Jane Frances de Chantal was born of a noble Burgundian family in 1572, happily married with six children, and tragically widowed, aged twenty-eight, in the eighth year of her marriage. She met Francis de Sales in 1604, and being attracted to his vision and spirituality, and recognising a true and holy kindred spirit, came under his spiritual direction. She moved to Annecy in 1610, where her desire for monastic life was finally realised with the co-founding, with St

Basilica of the Visitation.

Francis, of the Order of Visitandines. She died in Moulins, aged sixty-nine, in 1641, some nineteen years after St Francis, having already overseen the founding of 87 Visitandine monasteries. She was canonised in 1767 by Pope Clement XIII. Her feast is celebrated on 12th August. Today, there are over 165 Visitandine monasteries throughout the world.

Pilgrim Places in Annecy

Basilica of the Visitation: The slim, elegant Basilica of the Visitation, with its graceful tower and needle-point spire, sits serenely on a hill-top dominating the town – from where there are wide and open views of the surrounding mountains, the town and the lake. It was built between 1922 and 1930, as the convent church for the Visitandine monastery on the hill, being consecrated in 1949. In the two side altars rest the remains of St Francis and St Jane; both are in the matching style of impressionist, full-sized recumbent figures, in gleaming brushed brass – dignified, powerfully understated, and very moving. Their lives are vividly depicted, down each side of the church, by bright stained glass windows. A small shop run by the Sisters, and a museum are beside the Basilica; a café is on site. The Basilica is a lovely place to get above the hubbub of the town, to sit and take in the view, or to contemplate and pray in peace.

Back down in the town:

Church of St Francis de Sales: Overlooking one of the waterways, this conventional looking church, with a flat-fronted façade, was built for Jane de Chantal in 1612 and consecrated by Francis de Sales in 1617 as the Visitation Order's first monastery. The church has a light, spacious feel to it, with some interesting side chapels, in one of which is a picture of the death of St Joseph – a subject to which perhaps one never gives much thought until confronted with it. There is also a statue of the Black Madonna and a gilded wooden statue of St Jane de Chantal. The church serves the Italian colony of Annecy.

Church of St Maurice: St Maurice is the patron saint of Annecy, and this church dedicated to him was built in 1442 by the Dominicans. It is where St Francis de Sales made his First Holy Communion, and his Confirmation in 1575. A large, wide, single nave church, typical of a 'preaching order', in which my first impression on entering was 'hugely humble, and humbly huge'. Marvellously unfussy, from its plain ochre coloured walls, simple vaulted roof, and huge, gleaming stone flags worn smooth by a million footfalls – a holy, tranquil place, graced by a million prayers.

Cathedral of St Peter: Well into the old quarter, where you tend to come across it suddenly, rather than see it from a distance, is the Cathedral built in 1535 for the Franciscans, in Gothic style. It is where St Francis de Sales was ordained, and subsequently exercised his episcopacy. It has a rough, plain front façade, built with massive stone blocks. Inside, it is solid and lofty, with huge pillars and arches. It consists of three naves with ornate side altars. Bright, lively stained glass windows light the apse, with high windows letting in light for the rest of the church. The cathedral sports an immense organ, which by chance I was lucky enough to hear being played when I visited.

Our Lady of Joy: At the top end of the old quarter, by a narrow canal, is Notre Dame de Liesse – Our Lady (Cause of our) Joy. This church was built in 1851 on the site of a former church, of which the bell tower remains. On entry, my first impression: 'Dramatic!', but in a surprising and pleasing sense. A large, effective, glass-fronted narthex leads into a wide, three-naved church of solid, smooth-faced stone. It has an amazing columned, temple-like arrangement of the high altar, dramatically lit and back-lit, with a lustrous Madonna and Child prominent in the centre. The dramatic effect is further increased by the light pouring in from the plain glass crown of the neat dome immediately over the shallow transept. Rose windows, in a modern idiom, are set in each end of the transept, whilst more conventional stained glass windows go down the sides. Large, striking Stations of the Cross adorn the church. A striking church, not easily forgotten.

Grouped closely together is a **statue of St Francis de Sales** outside the **convent of the Sisters of St Joseph of Annecy**, which was the second monastery of the Visitation, founded by St Jane de Chantal in 1634, and the **Gallery House and Chapel** in which Jane de Chantal lived and from where the Visitation Order was founded. If you contact the Sisters of St Joseph at the convent you should be able to have access to the Gallery House and Chapel.

CHATEAUNEUF-DE-GALAURE

"Many people came to visit Marthe during her lifetime to seek her advice and counsel. In utter simplicity and often with a great sense of humour, she would chat with them. It was extremely rare for her to talk about herself. Her concern and compassion were always directed toward her guests...."

Henri Nouwen on Marthe Robin

Chateauneuf is in the Department of Drôme, some 50 miles south of Lyon, and just a few miles east of the A7/E15. It is a fairly sizeable, unremarkable, typical 'crossroads' French village. Buried deep in the countryside, it sits very comfortably in the lee of some high hills to the north, with the small River Galaure running through.

You are unlikely to find it on any endorsed pilgrim itinerary for France, for as yet, it is not formally approved as a place of 'official' pilgrimage by the Church. However, pilgrims do come here privately to pay their respects to Marthe Robin, stigmatic and mystic, who was born, lived and died here – in our times – in acute lifelong suffering and obscurity. Her legacy, however, is manifestly obvious in this village, with the substantial buildings of her foundation, the Foyers of Charity, which has since spread throughout the world.

Marthe Robin

A full account of Marthe Robin is given in the CTS booklet '*A Chosen Soul*'. She was born in an isolated farm in the hills just above Chateauneuf, in 1902, the sixth child of a farming family. She died in the same farmhouse 78 years later, in 1981, having been bedridden, almost totally paralysed for most of her life, and latterly, partially blind. At the onset of her gradually debilitating illness, aged 25, she unconditionally gave her suffering to Christ, asking Him to "receive the sacrifice that each day and at every moment I offer you in silence". French philosopher Jean Guitton said of her, after their meeting, "She was a peasant of the French countryside, who for thirty years took neither food nor drink, nourishing herself on the Eucharist alone, and every Friday she relived the pains of the Passion of Jesus through her stigmata. A woman who perhaps was the most unusual, most extraordinary and disconcerting of our age, but whom, even in the age of television, remained unknown to the public, buried in a profound silence".

Her mystical experiences soon gathered credence, and for much of her life visitors came to her from all over France seeking consolation and advice, including many priests. She persuaded her parish priest to start and open a church school for the village, which today is still in the village, but now in the form of three large, thriving, separate schools – primary and secondary, one for boys, one for girls, and a Technical College, with a combined total of about 1100 pupils from the local area and beyond, all benefiting from the inspiration given by the community members of the Foyers of Charity.

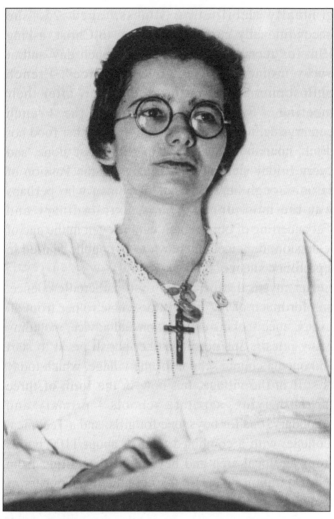

Marthe Robin.

Father Finet, a visiting priest from Lyons, had his life changed by his first encounter with her, resulting in an extraordinary partnership, whereby Marthe's wishes and instructions, inspired by her encounters with the Lord, were carried out by Fr Finet. The principal of these was the founding of a lay religious community, led by a priest, as the Foyers of Charity. Their sole mission is to give residential retreats to lay people of all ages, including families and priests, in an effort to renew the Faith and the Church. From very humble beginnings the Foyer's large suite of buildings now occupy the heights overlooking the village, and from here another 75 Foyers have been established, worldwide. Efforts are currently underway to establish the first Foyer in England.

Marthe is seen as an exceptional agent for renewal of spirituality and momentum within the Church, and has been the inspiration for many of today's New Movements. Her cause for Beatification is now with the Sacred Congregation for the Causes of the Saints in Rome, and is proceeding 'normally'. As such she is designated at the first stage of the process as 'Servant of God'.

Foyer

Members of the Foyer at Chateauneuf, although not geared to handling influxes of pilgrims, will welcome visitors who want to find out more about their work and Marthe Robin. Their imposing site above the village houses a large complex of buildings: the girls' school, a retreat centre accommodating up to 120 retreatants, housing for retired people, and the large, impressive modern church, built to accommodate the increasing numbers who worship here. You may also get directions to make the delightful mile or so country walk up to the Robins' farm at Moilles on the high ground above.

Ferme Robin

The small, neat farmhouse where Marthe spent her life has been preserved very much as it was during her life. The approach on the narrow country roads is discreetly marked with green signs *'Ferme Robin'*. Whether walking or driving, there are glorious, wide-open views of the surrounding countryside. The farm is set back from the road, surrounded by fields and orchards. Parking is available, and it has its own verdant gardens, offering the opportunity for some peaceful moments.

You will enter the house through the homely, family kitchen, with its original free-standing wood stove – still in use – pine furniture and imposing grandfather clock. Members of the Foyer live and work here, and in welcoming you, will prepare you for the focus of your pilgrimage: a quiet period of reflection and prayer in Marthe's bedroom, just off the kitchen – again, exactly as it was during her life.

The room is small and dimly lit, with two or three chairs placed for pilgrims round Marthe's divan bed. What may strike you immediately is that the divan is not full length – it was actually especially made for her, as through her paralysis, her legs were permanently drawn up under her body. There is an air of utter peace and tranquility about this place. There is also an air of utter normality in a room where a holy person lived their life – the pictures, statues and knick-knacks spread about so that she could constantly see them. Dominating, immediately above her bed, is the picture of Mary Mediatrix, the picture that Fr Finet brought to her at their first meeting, and from this inspiration of Our Lady, triggered the chain of events leading to the Foyers.

Many thousands of people passed through this room during her life, seeking her wise counsel, her inspiration and her intercession. Many countless thousands have done the same since her death, and continue to do so.

Saint-Bonnet-de-Galaure

The next village from Chateauneuf is Saint Bonnet, the parish in which the Robin family worshipped and where Marthe was christened. The small cemetery set back from the road is where Marthe is buried. A simple, inscribed, black marble tombstone, bedecked with flowers, marks her final resting place on earth – another peaceful place in which to ponder her life and outcome. You will also notice the large Technical College, run by the Foyers, on the outskirts of the village.

"Plunge in to the love of the Good Lord. A soul isn't pleasing to God because it is without sin, but because it believes in His mercy and abandons itself to His love in all confidence."

Marthe Robin

La Salette

"She wept all the time that she spoke to us... I clearly saw her tears, they flowed and flowed unceasingly".

High in the alpine pasture of the French Alps lies the Shrine and Sanctuary to Our Lady of La Salette. It is some 60 miles due south of Grenoble, off the N85. It is a gloriously remote and tranquil place, with spectacular views of the surrounding valleys and mountains, where, away from the immediate surrounds of the Sanctuary, you only hear piercing

La Salette.

birdsong and the hushing of small mountain streams as they bustle on down the mountainside. Although remote, it is easily accessible by car, up some very hair-pin bends, and there is very reasonable – in quality and price – pilgrim accommodation and facilities at the site.

Our Lady of La Salette

Our Lady appeared here in 1846 to two young shepherd children. Her message to humankind was one of turning away from sin and seeking repentance and conversion. She also made prophesies of war and famine, and imparted secrets to the seers. Many healing miracles have been directly attributed to Our Lady of La Salette. Despite the controversies of the seers' subsequent lives, the apparition is held as authentic by the Church, and La Salette has many devotees, attracting many pilgrims.

The Salette Cross, reported by the seers as being worn by Our Lady, is quite distinctive, hanging round her neck by its heavy chain, and adorned by hammer and pincers on each arm of the cross. One of the other enduring fruits of the apparition is the existence of the Missionaries and Sisters of La Salette, working in many places worldwide.

Basilica

In swift recognition of the validity of the apparition, the Basilica was built between 1852 and 1865. With its twin, square, flanking towers it is an imposing building, standing in stolid, angular contrast to this spectacular, soft, pastoral setting. It is large and quite austere inside: the rough stone wall-facings contrasting with the graceful, grey-marbled Byzantine columns supporting a Romanesque-style vaulted ceiling. Vibrant stained glass windows are at the middle level, whilst below, the smaller windows are more subtle, and more detailed in muted pastel colours. Around the walls are very striking Stations of the Cross, set in a modern, impressionistic style on irregular quarry-slate slabs.

The apse mural portrays a powerful, striking Christ as Pantocrator, with a strangely intriguing asymmetrical face, from which issues a bold, challenging gaze, and on which one side is the shadow of the Cross. There is a beautiful, serene, white marble statue of Madonna and Child above the high altar. Part of the large pilgrim complex also houses a modern, semicircular, be-windowed chapel looking out onto the mountains, for groups to hold prayer sessions or celebrate Mass.

Outside you can trace the seers' footsteps in the **Valley of the Apparition**: there are two Ways of the Cross, and three statue groups depicting the stages of the apparition. Several hiking trails lead off from the Sanctuary into the surrounding area; there is a small oratory on an adjacent hilltop, built in 1857. It is a beautiful, peaceful place where you can immerse yourself in Our Lady's presence, surrounded by God's most natural and grand-scale handiwork.

'Let yourselves be reconciled with God'
(Mt 5:23 f.; Mk 11:24 f.; 2 Cor 5:18 ff; Eph 2:15)

LAUS

"It is my wish that a church be erected here in honour of my Dearly Beloved Son. Here, many sinners will understand the error of their ways; here, too, you will often see me."

About an hour's drive further south from La Salette, just southeast from Gap off the N85, is the **Sanctuary to Our Lady of Laus**, in a lower, more rugged alpine setting, but one of rural peace and tranquility. St-Etienne-de-Laus is one of the oldest (1664) but least known apparitions sites of Our Lady in France, probably, and intriguingly, because it was not formally accepted by the Church until May 2008, although it has had the local Bishop's approval since 1665. Many miracles have been witnessed here, and many pilgrims have been coming ever since the apparitions were reported.

Once again, Our Lady chose to appear to a young, illiterate shepherd girl, Benôite Rencurel, and continued to do so for the remaining fifty four years of her life. Our Lady's message was one of conversion, particularly through reconciliation. As with Bernadette, she also asked for a church to be built on the site, even prescribing design and dimension. It has been described as one of 'the most hidden and powerful shrines of Europe'. Very pleasant pilgrim accommodation is available, and the Sanctuary is served by the lovely Benedictine Sisters of Montmartre.

Basilica

Work swiftly began in constructing the simple, sturdy basilica in 1666. Inside it has a single, wide nave, the side walls adorned with large frescoes depicting aspects of Benôite's life. The altar is in the form of a striking *baldacchino* arrangement, part of the original *'Bon Rencontre'* church. Its gleaming, white stone altar and statue of Our Lady, contrasts with the richly adorned canopy with its dark green, marbled supporting pillars.

Hillside Apparition scene, Pindreau.

Close to the tabernacle, but at waist height, burns the sanctuary lamp, announcing the presence of Our Lord. Our Lady told Benôite that the oil from the sanctuary lamp, if applied in faith and through prayer to her Son, would cure the physically and spiritually sick. The oil can be used by pilgrims direct from the lamp, or obtained (for a voluntary donation) from the Pilgrim Office, to take home. Numerous reports have testified to healings. Benôite's mortal remains lie below ground level at the foot of the altar. Continuous adoration takes place in the **Benôite Oratory**, close to the basilica.

Outside there are many way-marked *randonnées* or walking paths, mostly associated with the Sanctuary. One which is particularly recommended is the 45 or so minute walk through woods to the hillside at Pindreau, where there is a **bronze statue group** depicting the apparitions – overlooking the peaceful valley.

LALOUVESC

Buried in a myriad of "D" roads in the lovely scenic mountains of the Ardèche, some 40 miles south of Saint-Etienne, is the village of Lalouvesc, the last resting place of **St John Francis Regis** (1597–1640). St John Francis was a Jesuit, noted for his ceaseless and tireless work on evangelising missions in remote and dangerous areas of the Vivarais and the Velay,

OSSEMENTS DE SAINT REGIS

The reliquary of St John Francis.

helping wayward women, and tending to the sick, the poor and prisoners. He died in Lalouvesc, having struggled through winter storms to get there, catching pneumonia in the process, but insisting with carrying on with his mission. He was an inspiration to the Curé of Ars, who visited his tomb in 1804, and who one can see modelled his own ministry on his. On his deathbed the Curé said of St John Francis, "Everything good that I have done, I owe to him". He was canonised in 1737.

There also came to Lalouvesc **St Thérèse Couderc** (1805–1885) in 1826 to join the community known as the Religious of St Regis. The community later divided into two branches with Thérèse being the first Mother Superior of the Religious of the Cenacle which primarily served women who came on retreat – a new concept in 19th century France. She moved round various convents in France preaching her message of 'goodness' and surrender to the divine. Thérèse was canonised in 1970, and her message still lives on in the many communities of the Sisters of the Cenacle round the world.

In Lalouvesc you will find:
Basilica of St Regis: handsome, ornate, twin-towered basilica, built between 1864 and 1877. The basilica houses the reliquary of St John Francis in a striking

setting beside the altar, and his life is depicted through the stained glass windows of the church.

Chapel of St Regis, previously the church presbytery, is where St John Francis died, and next to it is the **museum and diorama**. **The Miraculous Fountain** from which it is said St John Francis drank when he arrived on his last mission here, and to which miraculous cures have been attributed, is between the basilica and the Chapel. There is an attractive **Pilgrims' Park and Way of the Cross** within walking distance of the basilica. **The Chapel and convent of St Thérèse Couderc** welcomes pilgrims visiting during the day. The Chapel contains the incorrupt body of St Thérèse.

LE PUY-EN-VELAY

Le Puy-en-Velay is about 80 miles south of Clermont Ferrand in the Haute Loire, on the N102. In pilgrim terms is a fascinating place to visit. To some, as it was for me, it is one of the principal starting places for the walking pilgrimage to the Shrine of St James at Santiago de Compostela, some 900 miles away (see CTS booklet *Santiago de Compostela*). To others it is a fascinating combination of geology and architecture, particularly the small **church of St Michael the**

Archangel perching precariously, up many steps, on a rugged, high, volcanic plug of rock.

But mostly, it is about Our Lady. Tradition has it that she appeared to a gravely ill woman in the 1st century, curing her, which led to a Marian shrine and altar being raised, and latterly the cathedral being built on that spot. Then there is a copy of the ebony statue of one of the famous 'Black Madonnas' brought back by James I of Aragon from the Holy Land in the cathedral, which is the subject of veneration – one cannot help but give a wry smile to the Infant Jesus, peeking rather cheekily out from His mother's robe!

The **12th century cathedral** itself, dedicated to Our Lady, is described as architecturally 'audacious and picturesque', being in a Romanesque style with Moorish elements, and having a distinctive entry, after the ascent of many stairs. Above the cathedral and dominating the town, mounted on another volcanic outcrop, is the huge, hollow, bronze **statue of Our Lady** – an edifice that seems to defy all health and safety regulations, because one can climb all the way up inside and look out over the town from the top of her head!

The church of St Michael the Archangel.

PYRENEES AND
 PROVENCE

LOURDES

"I am the Immaculate Conception."

Lourdes must be one of the best known pilgrim destinations in modern Christendom: certainly a vast number of Catholics round the world will have heard of it, and what the name stands for. For it was here, in 1858, that Our Lady appeared to an impoverished, teenage girl – Marie-Bernarde Soubirous, more commonly known as Bernadette – imparting her message of poverty, penance and prayer, and ultimately, hope and healing. Since then, pilgrims have been drawn here by that message, in their millions – seeking that healing and hope, and many experiencing conversion.

Saint Bernadette

Bernadette was born in January 1844, the eldest of nine children, of whom five survived beyond childhood. She was a sickly and asthmatic child, having survived a bout of cholera. The family lived in grindingly impoverished conditions, and as eldest child and daughter, she had to take on the role of 'second mother', while her mother worked. All this deprived her of any regular education, and also kept her away from her catechism classes.

On the 11th of February, 1858, Bernadette was out gathering firewood in the area of the Massabielle cave by the River Gave, when she "heard a noise something like a gust of wind". On looking up she saw in the Grotto, surrounded by "a gentle light", a beautiful young woman making a welcoming gesture. This was the first of eighteen apparitions, which went on until 16th July 1858. The most significant was the sixteenth apparition on the 25th March, the feast of the Annunciation, when after three previous occasions, Bernadette again asked who she was. "I am the Immaculate Conception", was the reply – words that had no significance for Bernadette, but had a huge impact on the hitherto sceptical parish priest: for they were the words that summed up (and confirmed) the dogma of the Immaculate Conception, pronounced by Pope Pius IX four years earlier.

In another significant apparition (the third) Our Lady told Bernadette, "I do not promise to make you happy in this world, but in the other", a presage of the suffering in her future life. The ninth apparition was also important: then Our Lady told Bernadette to dig in the damp earth of the cave, uncovering the spring that ever since has produced some 27,000 gallons of water daily. Reports of miracles associated with bathing with the water soon started coming in; whilst some may have been wishful thinking or rumour, two were accepted by the Church after full investigation – a woman's paralysed arm being cured, and eyesight being restored to a stonemason blinded in one eye.

In January 1862, after lengthy investigation, the Bishop of Tarbes declared the apparitions as bearing the characteristics of truth, and worthy of belief by the faithful. Bernadette spent the next eight years in Lourdes, boarding at the Hospice, helping to tend the sick, and catching up with her education.

In July 1866, she left Lourdes, never to return, joining the Sisters of Charity, at their Mother House in Nevers, Burgundy. Here she lived out the rest of her short life in enclosure – a life of prayer, experiencing physical, and at times, spiritual suffering – working mainly in the convent infirmary and sacristy. Her health deteriorated, with distressing asthma attacks, and, the tuberculosis in the bones of her knee finally took hold. She died on 16 April 1879, aged 35. She was canonised in 1933 by Pope Pius XI. Today, her incorrupt body lies in the convent chapel in Nevers, where the faithful come to seek her intercession (see the chapter on Burgundy). The feast day of Our Lady of Lourdes is 11th February, and St Bernadette's is on 16th April.

Lourdes

The town of Lourdes sits in the lush, green, northern foothills of the Pyrenees. It is some 60 kms south of the spa town of Pau, and about 170 kms east from the hedonistic seaside resort of Biarritz on the Atlantic coast. It had a strategic role in the Middle Ages, as shown by the 11th century fortress commanding the heights of the Lavedan valley. In Bernadette's day it was quite isolated, the local people – Bigourdanians – speaking their own version of Occitan (*langue d'oc*), and the town having a reputation for recalcitrance to any authority, including the Church – in fact the diocesan authorities reportedly "dread the very mention of its name"! Witchcraft and sorcery also pervaded the area.

Today, the town as a whole, is a busy, international destination, with many thousands of pilgrims visiting daily. At its heart is the Domain – some 52 hectares of beautifully kept and cared-for grounds and buildings. And whilst the Domain is surrounded by shop-upon-shop selling religious articles catering for every taste, and phalanxes of hotels, cafes and restaurants, and despite the crowds, throughout the Domain there still permeates an aura of calm and dignity, and there are always quiet corners and spaces. The noticeable presence of the sick, infirm and disabled demonstrates

The Grotto - Lourdes.

the role of Lourdes, and is manifest by the way they are treated as the Domain's 'VIPs'.

Domain

Dominating the Domain is the graceful, needle-pointed spire of the basilica, with its two flanking towers, and the embracing arms of the two large semicircular staircases coming down on to the concourse (Rosary Square) to welcome and admit pilgrims. The seemingly single church is in fact three: the exquisite, small and intimate **Crypt**, opened in 1866, was the first church to be built in response to Our Lady's request: "Go tell the priests to have a chapel built here"; then, in response to the growing numbers of pilgrims, the **Basilica of the Immaculate Conception** which was consecrated in 1871; and then below the Crypt, the neo-Byzantine styled **Rosary Basilica**, finished in 1889.

But at the very heart of the Domain is its intense spiritual focus: the **Grotto of Massabielle**, the cave by the side of the River Gave, where Our Lady appeared to Bernadette. The iconic statue of Our Lady of Lourdes is in the crevice above – exactly where she appeared to Bernadette; underneath, her words, spoken in the local patois, *'Que soy era Immaculada Councepciou'*, words that Bernadette at the time did not understand, nor had heard before. Inside the

Grotto, there is a small altar, and an ever-burning pyramid of candles. Pilgrims sit, stand or kneel in rapt prayer and reflection.

Around the Domain there are many other places of worship and prayer: the **Chapel of St Joseph** by St Michael's Gate, the large modern **church of St Bernadette** across the river and opposite the Grotto, a small **Adoration Chapel** immediately next door; a large Adoration Tent in the **Meadow (*Prairie*)** used for busy periods, and the vast, modern underground **Basilica of St Pius X** capable of holding over 20,000 pilgrims. The **Chapel of Reconciliation** on the main boulevard approaching the basilicas has 48 confessionals where the Sacrament of Reconciliation is administered in every major European language. On the wooded hillside, just outside the Domain are the **Stations of the Cross**, with dramatic life-sized statues, covering an undulating 1,500 metre path. A more compact Stations, on the level, is available on the *Prairie* for the infirm.

Lastly – the **Immersion Baths** – which despite my scepticism and aversion to cold water, was the highlight of my experience at Lourdes. Here, within this rather nondescript building, you are reverently and prayerfully immersed in the waters of the spring that have flowed prodigiously since Our Lady's invitation to Bernadette to unearth it and, "Go drink of the spring and wash yourself there". I was oblivious to the cold water, and as our tour guide had predicted, I came out 'dry'. This amazing experience led me immediately into an encounter in which I very strongly felt the presence of Our Lady.

Outside the Domain, in the old town, is the easily accessible *cachot* – the cramped former prison cell where the Soubirous family lived; their former home, the **Boly Mill**, and the **Hospice** where Bernadette boarded and completed her education. A short excursion, or even walk, will take you to **Bartres** to see the sheepfold where Bernadette tended her flock, the Lagues household, where she lived part of her time as a child, and the parish church.

Events

There are two major, daily events held in the Domain. The first, in the early evening and aimed specifically at those who seek healing, is the procession of the Blessed Sacrament to, and the **Blessing of the Sick** in, the St Pius X Basilica (April–October). It is a moving experience pervaded with fervent prayer, faith and hope. Lastly, there is the candlelit **Rosary procession** from the Grotto to Rosary Square in front of the basilicas. It is a vast sea of twinkling lights, waves of prayer and song, seemingly from all nations of the world, rising heavenward. This is a great living and lasting testament to the instruction Our Lady gave to Bernadette, "Tell the priests and people to come here in procession". After the procession the last Mass of the day is held at the Grotto at 11pm.

An **International Mass** is held on Sundays and Wednesdays mornings (April–October) in the St Pius X Basilica – a great gathering of the international Church family. There are generous opportunities for **Eucharistic Adoration** round the Domain.

Healing miracles

Those early miracles soon established Lourdes as a place for the sick – physical, mental or spiritual – to come and seek healing. Whilst there is little doubt that many thousands experience healing of some sort after their visit to Lourdes, only 67 so far have been pronounced by the Church as miraculous. This may be because many people are just content to give thanks to God and keep their experience to themselves, their family and friends. For the process of declaring miraculous healing is extremely rigorous, involving three separate stages of medical scrutiny by boards of medical specialists who are completely independent from the Church. Having passed the objective medical stages, the process still has to undergo canonical scrutiny by the local bishop, before it can be declared miraculous.

The latest, and sixty-seventh miracle to be recognised was in November 2005. Anna Santaniello, a 41 year old Italian lady, was cured of severe heart disease and associated debilitating symptoms, after being bathed in the waters in 1952 whilst on pilgrimage. She was 93 years old when she died.

"My weapons are prayer and sacrifice, and I will keep them until my last breath. Then, finally, the weapon of suffering will fall from my hand. But the weapon of prayer will follow me to heaven, where it will be even more powerful."

St Bernadette

ROCAMADOUR

In the Lot department, about 110 miles north of Toulouse, just east off the A20/E9, is the dramatic, mediaeval village of Rocamadour, dizzyingly stepping up the cliff-side of the gorge through which flows the River Alzou. Because of its picturesque and appealing setting it is a popular tourist destination; however, pilgrims have been coming here long before the tourists, either staging through on their way to Santiago de Compostela, and/or coming to venerate the *Vierge Noire* – **the Black Madonna of Rocamadour**, and Saint Amadour. The views from

Rocamadour.

the plateau-top are spectacular, and the village, churches and chateau when lit at night present a beautiful and ethereal sight. For the gastronomically inclined Rocamadour also gives its name to a well known goats' cheese.

Our Lady of Rocamadour

The first recorded mention of the carved walnut statue of the Black Virgin being venerated in Rocamadour is 1105. It is estimated that there are at least 180 mediaeval *Vierge Noires* in France – the colour black being attributed to the dark patina of the statues, accrued over the centuries from candle soot, but there are other, more esoteric theories about the colouring: one is that it stems from the Old Testament verse from Song of Songs 1:5, 'I am black but lovely, daughters of Jerusalem…'.

The origin of this statue is thought to be 9th century, although it is inevitably described by legend as having been brought here by St Amadour in the first century. The chapel to Our Lady has been rebuilt several times over the centuries, but through all the vicissitudes of the turbulent past, the statue has remained intact. The statue of the seated Madonna with Child is illuminated, placed above the ornate altar, shining out to pilgrims in the subdued lighting of the chapel.

Saint Amadour

In 1166 an incorrupt body was discovered in a cliff-side cave. Its identity was unknown, but assumed to be that of a hermit, soon assuming the name 'Amator' – lover (of God) – from which evolved the name Rocamadour: rock of the lover. Such a find fuelled further speculation that this man was Zaccheus, the tax collector from St Luke's Gospel, and husband of St Veronica, drawing medieval pilgrims to this site. The relics were destroyed during the Religious Wars, but the cave where his body was discovered is still evident in the cliff-side adjacent to the church square, and remaining relics are housed in the Crypt of St Amadour.

Cité Religieuse

Cité Religeuse is the collection of seven churches and chapels grouped together round the church square, which is reached after a climb of 216 steps – *Escalier des Pelerins* – (or by lift if you prefer) from the village below. The churches consist of the 11th–13th century, Romanesque-Gothic style **Basilica of St Sauveur**, interconnecting with the **Chapel of Our Lady**, and which are generally open to the public; the **Crypt of St Amadour** and the **chapel of St Michael**, in which there are 12th century frescoes, and are accessible only through a guided tour, and the three small chapels of St Anne, St Blaise and St John the Baptist, which are not open to the public. Also around the square is a **museum** and bookshop, and kiosk for booking tours of the site. There is a short tunnel, leading to the **Way of the Cross**, which takes you up to the chateau and ramparts on the plateau overlooking the gorge. There is also a lift.

Many miracles of healing during the Middle Ages were recorded as having been attributed to the intercession of the *Vierge Noir* and St Amadour, and as evidenced by the many testimonial articles left in the churches. Popes, saints and kings have made their pilgrimage to this remote spot – including Eleanor of Aquitaine, Henry II of England, Louis XI, Saints Dominic, Bernard and Anthony of Padua, and the French composer Francis Poulenc, who composed his 'Litanies of the Black Virgin' in thanksgiving for his religious conversion whilst staying in Rocamadour.

The sanctuaries were pillaged and burned in the 16th century by the Huguenots. It was not until the mid 19th century that a priest who had been miraculously cured through the intercession of the *Vierge Noire*, and a priest colleague, started gathering funds and resources to restore the shrines.

CONQUES

95 or so kms east of Rocamadour, on the D901 in another remote area of the Massif Central, is the small, perfectly preserved mediaeval town of Conques. It was, and still is, a significant stopping-off point for pilgrims trudging along the Way of St James to Santiago de Compostela. I passed through it as a pilgrim on my walk to Santiago, and was very impressed by the way that the more garish aspects of tourism had been kept well at bay, thereby retaining the town's medieval character, making it easier to picture this charming small town as it was those many centuries ago.

Initially a hermit called Dadon founded his spiritual retreat here in the 8th century, and gradually, with the gathering of a group of followers, a Carolingian church was built, and was later endowed by Charlemagne's son. It was only after the relics of Saint Foy (Saint Faith) were brought to the abbey here that it started becoming a desirable pilgrim stopping-off point.

Saint Foy

Saint Foy was born in Agen in the west of France of a prominent pagan family in around 290. Legend says that, aged twelve, she secretly converted to Christianity. When this inevitably came to light she was brought before the Roman Governor Dacien, noted for his persecution of Christians. She would not recant her faith, and to show an example to other Christians in the area, she was tortured and beheaded in 303 – a young virgin martyr. Rather than suppress Christianity, this inspired more who followed her to faith and some to martyrdom. Her relics were hidden by the community of the faithful, who met annually to venerate them amongst reports of miracles being wrought through their intercession. After Constantine's Edict of Milan in 313, her relics were incorporated in a small golden statue and displayed in the church in Agen, where for five hundred years pilgrims came to venerate her.

In a strange twist to the tale of Saint Foy, the monks at Conques, wanting to attract more pilgrims (and hence wealth and distinction), conspired to appropriate the reliquary from Agen, which they successfully achieved. Quite how the authorities at Agen reacted to this unorthodox 'translation' does not seem to be recorded, other than the fact that the relics have resided at Conques since the end of the 9th century!

"The crowd of people prostrating themselves on the ground was so dense it was impossible to kneel down... When they saw it for the first time, all in gold and sparkling with precious stones and looking like a human face, the majority of the

The Abbey of Ste Foy.

peasants thought that the statue was really looking at them and answering their prayers with her eyes."

An account by clergyman Bernard D'Angers of pilgrims

before the reliquary in 1010

The Abbey of Saint Foy

The original Carolingian church was demolished in the 11th century to make way for the sturdy, but starkly elegant Romanesque abbey that still stands today. Construction started under the direction of the Benedictine abbot Odolric, and was completed in the late 12th century. The subsequent years saw some changes, mostly brought about by the ravages of the Huguenots in the 16th century, and, following the French Revolution it was abandoned and fell into ruinous disrepair. This had one beneficial effect, as in 1837 work commenced to restore the abbey, and in 1873 the local bishop installed the Premonstratensians (the White Canons) to run the church; two years later they discovered Saint Foy's reliquary, which had been hidden from sight during the Religious Wars of the 14th century. Interest in the abbey and Saint Foy picked up again. Saint Foy's relics are now displayed in the museum next to the cloister. The reliquary is claimed as the only surviving example of the statue-reliquary that was common in the Middle Ages.

The church inside is unadorned, with plain stonework facings, and sturdy columns each side of the central nave. There is an ambulatory round the be-pillared sanctuary, with side chapels off, in the Cluniac style, including the all-important chapel of St James for the Santiago pilgrims, and Saint Foy. The modern, stained glass windows were installed in 1995. The exterior is bluff and fortress-like, dominated by the three powerful towers topped by the tapering spired roofs. Probably the most striking feature of this church, and for which it is best known, is the extensive, detailed, beautifully carved tympanum over the west door, depicting in graphic detail, the Last Judgement. It was sculpted in the early 12th century – some of its original pre-Reformation colouring shows faintly through.

LA SAINTE-BAUME

"For this reason I tell you that her sins, many as they are, have been forgiven her, because she has shown such great love."

Lk 9:47

Mary Magdalene

The Sainte Baume Massif, just to the east of Marseille, is a huge curiosity of limestone outcrop – the result of a geological 'inversion', which led to this 10 km-long ridge being thrust up from the depths of the Plan D'Aup plateau. It is here, in a large cave (*la Sainte-Baume* – the Holy Cave), high up on the north side of the Massif, that tradition in France has it that Mary Magdalene spent her last years. It claims that she was cast afloat from the Holy Land in a boat without sails and oars, along with Martha, Lazarus, Maximin and others. Divine Providence is said to have guided the boat to landfall on the shores of Provence, at Saintes-Maries-de-la-Mer, near Arles. She evangelised in and around the Marseilles area, eventually retiring to an eremitical life in this cave, until her life's end.

There has been a shrine in this cave, dedicated to Mary Magdalene, for centuries: in the care of the Cassianites from the 5th century, of the Benedictines in the 11th century, passing to the Dominicans in the 13th century, who are the present-day custodians. It has been a noted place of pilgrimage since early days – from those pilgrims who passed through on their way to Santiago de Compostela, to Popes and many French Kings and Queens, who followed the path – the *Chemins des Rois* – up the mountainside to the church inside the cave. Although the church suffered internal desecration during the French Revolution and other upheavals, it must be the only 'church' in

France that still retains its totally original form – as in effect the walls, floor and roof are formed by the cave.

Access to the cave is by a 50 minute or so walk along the ever-ascending track from the nearest roadside car parks, initially through an ancient, predominantly evergreen forest, with tall, moss-bedecked trunks and cool, all-enveloping overhead canopy. It is a sublime walk – through utter tranquillity and an immensity that no man-made cathedral can match, accompanied only by the soft soughing of the leaves overhead, and piercing, crystal-clear birdsong, seemingly amplified by this mighty cathedral. Along one of the routes are Stations of the Cross, ending in a powerful sculpted, polychrome Calvary scene near the cave.

Church in the cave

The final approach is up 150 stairs, ending on the flagged, level parvis in front of the church. The views from up here are breathtaking – looking out across the Provençal countryside, or dizzyingly along and up the cliff edge. On the edge of the parvis – effectively the cliff edge – is a large, dramatic, bronze-cast Pietà, with Mary Magdalene hunched on the ground by Jesus's feet. To the right of the parvis is the small monastery building, clinging to the cliff face, that houses the priests who stay and tend the shrine. There is nothing more evocative than looking up at that cliff face late at night and seeing a lonely light shining out, or hearing the distant, plaintive tolling of the monastery bell, calling out the Liturgy of Hours. To the left of the parvis is a small gift shop and pilgrim shelter.

The only concession to natural structure is the enclosing stonework of the back wall and entry door to the church. The cave is sizeable. It is chilly inside. In moments of quiet, the only accompaniment is the intermittent, musical plip-and-plop of dripping water. The main altar is on a stone-stepped podium, backed by a large arch-enclosed crucifix, below which Mary Magdalene kneels. To the left, fitting in with the natural shape of the cave, is the Blessed Sacrament side altar. There are many statues round the cave, which is at two levels, and a small, brightly-lit reliquary is inset on the right side of the main altar. Bright, vivid stained glass windows, depicting various stages of Mary Magdalene's life, adorn the rear wall. This is a beautiful place in which to worship and meditate, and genuine or not, it matters not – it is an authentic setting to inspire one to follow in Mary Magdalene's footsteps, if not literally, then certainly spiritually.

If you have time and the energy, it is worth the extra forty minutes plod up to the top of the Massif to St Pilon's chapel, where the view, including a glimpse of the Mediterranean, goes the full 360 degrees.

The Holy Cave.

This is another remote site, away from the rush of modern life, accessed up narrow, hair-pin roads, and set in harsh, but beautiful scenery. There is a hospitable pilgrim hostel with board and accommodation associated with the shrine, served by welcoming Dominican friars and sisters. In the hostel there is a lovely small chapel in which the Dominican community pray the Daily Office and celebrate Mass, to all of which pilgrims are welcome. The walls of the chapel are adorned with large, probably over-romanticised, but nonetheless beautiful and appealing frescoes of Mary Magdalene's life in France. As ever, in these scenic settings in France, there are extensive, well-marked walking trails throughout the region.

The nearby town of **St-Maximin-la-Ste-Baume** is also worth a visit, where, amongst doing other things, you can visit the impressive 13th century **Gothic basilica of Ste Marie Madeleine**, housing some of her relics.

"The story of Mary Magdalene reminds everyone of a fundamental truth: she is a disciple of Christ who, in the experience of human weakness, has had the humility to ask for his help, has been healed by him, and has followed him closely, becoming a witness of the power of his merciful love, which is stronger than sin and death."

Pope Benedict XVI

COTIGNAC

"This motherhood of Mary in the economy of grace lasts without interruption, from the consent which she gave in faith at the Annunciation, and which she unhesitatingly bore with under the cross, even to the perpetual consummation of all the elect."

Lumen Gentium 61-62

In the hills of Provence, just over an hour's drive north from Toulon, and well away from main roads, is the small town of Cotignac, set at the foot of a cliff and beside the River Cassolle. Another insignificant, anonymous place, had it not been for an unusual double blessing of two apparitions, firstly from Our Lady in 1519, and (separately and unconnected) a rare and brief apparition of St Joseph, in 1660.

Our Lady of Graces

In August 1519, Jean de la Baume, a woodcutter working alone in the hills overlooking the village, received an apparition of Our Lady, holding the Child Jesus, and flanked by St Bernard of Clairvaux, St Catherine of Alexander, and St Michael the Archangel. She had a simple message for Jean: "I am the Virgin Mary. Go and tell the clergy and the Consuls of Cotignac to build me a church on this place in the name of Our Lady of Graces, and that they should come in procession to receive the gifts which I wish to bestow."

Thinking it to be some hallucination, the woodcutter kept this to himself, but the next day Our Lady appeared to him again, repeating her message. This time Jean reported it to the village officials – and being known for his responsible and sober nature, he was believed. Work started almost immediately, and a church was built on the site of the apparition, but was soon outgrown by the number of visiting pilgrims. It was replaced by a sanctuary of about the same size as the existing church, completed by 1537, catering for the ever increasing numbers that had started heading for Cotignac and Our Lady of Graces.

The site continued to serve pilgrims over the years – but the story does not end there. The succession to Louis XIII was in doubt: his marriage to Anne of Austria in 1615 had not yet produced an heir during 22 years. An Augustinian friar, Brother Fiacre, based in Paris, was inspired by visions specifically of Our Lady of Graces to start praying for the marriage to bear fruit – which it did. Exactly nine months after Br Fiacre had completed the novena prescribed by Our Lady, Anne gave birth to a son, Louis Dieudonne

('Godgiven'), who succeeded his father as Louis XIV. In profound gratitude, Queen Anne kneeled before Br Fiacre. In a more public and significant gesture Louis XIII, in thanking God for events during his reign, made a Vow of Consecration, which in part stated, "To this end we have declared that taking the very holy and glorious Virgin Mary as special protectress of our kingdom, we particularly consecrate to her our own Self, the State, our Crown, and our subjects…".

The Revolution saw the church demolished and sold off in lots as building materials, and the hill-top lay bare and desolate for many years. Work on the new basilica started in the early 1950s, and is now complete.

The basilica is set in extensive, terraced grounds with fine views, and plenty of nooks and crannies in which to seek peace and quiet. The church displays a simple, robust dignity. A high vaulted roof, a wide, single nave, and bright, butter-coloured walls, contrast effectively with the royal blue, stippled ceiling. The original statue and picture of the apparition, which were hidden by the faithful during the Revolution, are on proud display. A small café and bookshop are available on site. There is a walking path (about 50 minutes) that takes you to the Monastery of St Joseph. By tradition, childless couples pray to Our Lady of Graces.

St Joseph

"Water is the sign, so essential in our faith, of our regeneration and of the new life risen for us in Christ's Easter. Here is brought to light St Joseph's role as powerful intercessor."

Mgr Gilles Barthe, pastoral letter February 1971

On the day in 1660 that Louis XIV's betrothed wife, Marie-Thérèse of Spain, entered France for the first time, the second supernatural appearance occurred in Cotignac. Gaspard Ricard, a 22 year old shepherd, was high up on the parched hillside on a stifling hot day with his flock. As he rested and pondered where to water the sheep, a tall, venerable man appeared by his side and gestured towards a nearby large boulder. "I am Joseph," said the stranger, "lift it and you will drink." Seeing Gaspard's hesitation, he repeated, "Lift it and you will drink." Moving the rock, fresh water immediately began to flow from underneath it. In turning to thank the stranger, he found no one there.

He immediately hastened back down to the village, reporting this strange encounter. On returning to the spot with many villagers, they saw this abundant new source of water, and on examining the boulder that Gaspard had so easily moved, it took eight men to shift it. The Consuls of Cotignac responded swiftly. A small chapel was built over the site, but soon proved inadequate to meet pilgrim numbers who started flocking there, so by 1663, a larger chapel was built and consecrated. Owing to its remote location, damage to this chapel was comparatively minimal during the Revolution, it being largely the same building as it is today.

This is another isolated and tranquil site, set high on the hillside. Benedictine Sisters serve the Sanctuary, and live in the convent next door. Pilgrims are welcome to attend Mass and their Liturgy of the Hours in the chapel. The little Grotto of St Joseph is outside and below the church on the left side, and is accessible at all hours. It is a lovely spot in which to pray, listening to the soft murmurings of that flowing spring. The water is available to pilgrims from the tap below. There have been many reported healings from this 'living water'. In an echo of his father's Consecration to Our Lady, and in acknowledgment of the connection that his father and mother, Queen Anne, had with Our Lady of Graces, Louis XIV consecrated himself and his kingdom to St Joseph.

Grotto of St Joseph.